Bristol & Clifton
SLAVE TRADE
TRAILS

Terry Townsend

TO MY WIFE CAROL

*who patiently and supportively worked with me
on every aspect of writing this book.*

First published in Great Britain in 2016

Copyright © Terry Townsend 2016

British Library Cataloguing-in-Publication Data
A CIP record for this title is available from the
British Library

ISBN 978 0 85710 104 4

PiXZ Books
Halsgrove House, Ryelands Business Park,
Bagley Road, Wellington, Somerset TA21 9PZ
Tel: 01823 653777
Fax: 01823 216796
email: sales@halsgrove.com

An imprint of Halstar Ltd, part of the
Halsgrove group of companies
Information on all Halsgrove titles is
available at: www.halsgrove.com

Printed and bound in China by
Everbest Printing Investment Ltd

CONTENTS

THE TRAILS
Beginning at...

ACKNOWLEDGEMENTS

Thanks for the encouragement and practical help
extended by Adrienne Bradney-Smith
and Brenda and Tony Stables

I am indebted to the scholarship of the Bristol team of
Madge Dresser, Caletta Jordan, Doreen Taylor,
Christine Eicklemann and David Small

RECOMMENDED FURTHER READING

Slavery Obscured
The Social History of the Slave Trade in Bristol
Madge Dresser

Pero
The Life of a Slave in Eighteenth-century Bristol
Christine Eickelmann and David Small

Slave Ship
A Human History
Marcus Rediker

A Respectable Trade
Philippa Gregory

PROLOGUE

Sitting comfortably in Bristol's Theatre Royal we anticipate the city's great historical drama. Cast in leading roles are former mayors and MPs of the municipality: Alleyne, Baillie, Colston, Daniels, Farr, Goldney, Hilhouse, Pinney etc. They will play the parts of merchants, shipbuilders, sugar refiners, linen and glass manufacturers and plantation owners.

The orchestra strikes up and the rising curtain reveals an assembly of elegant dancers. Ladies in beautiful ball gowns minuet with handsome partners in evening dress. We see Susanna James Montague, Jane Elizabeth Nusum, Lucretia Pearce Hall all stepping lightly with other mothers, sisters and daughters of Bristol's bourgeoisie.

Then, gradually from stage left, comes a sound like the dragging of chains. The noise increases and is augmented by pitiful wails. The spotlight picks out a group of naked Negroes, shuffling and bowed. Urged on by whips these wretched creatures are forced to dance to the music. They make a poor showing as they are hampered by iron fetters which have caused weeping sores round their ankles.

Programme notes show this scene to be a re-enactment of the enforced daily exercise on the deck of a slave ship from Africa bound for the Caribbean. After being crushed together for hours in the fetid below-decks world of the stinking vessel, the slaves require sharp persuasion from a 'cat-o'-nine-tails' before they will take part in the grotesque ballet.

The orchestra pit we are told represents the depths of the ocean and blessed release from the torture. But suicide by jumping overboard has been anticipated and rope netting has been stretched across the width of the stage. Some of the audience gasp and shift uneasily in their seats. Others rise to leave. The strangest part of this ghastly charade is that the wealthy ball-goers appear oblivious to the suffering of their fellow human beings with whom they share the stage.

'So enormous, so dreadful, so irremediable did the Trade's wickedness

appear that my own mind was completely made up for Abolition.

Let the consequences be what they would, I from this time determined

that I would never rest until I had effected its abolition.'

William Wilberforce

INTRODUCTION

For most of the eighteenth-century the city of Bristol, situated at the confluence of the Frome and Avon rivers, was Britain's leading port after London. This brought great trade and consequent wealth to certain of the city's inhabitants.

Much of the prosperity was built on the 'Triangular Trade', which exploited Atlantic sea lanes shaped by the powerful influence of winds and currents during the age of sail. In the classic example, trade goods were shipped from Bristol to the west coast of Africa and bartered for slaves. Many of these goods, including, alcohol, metalware, linen and glass were produced in the city and were traded for Negro men, women and children who had been captured by slave traders or bought from African chiefs.

On the second leg, or 'middle passage' of the ship's progress, slaves were transported across the Atlantic to work on plantations in the Caribbean Islands and New England. Those who survived the densely packed, filthy and brutal conditions

The harbour painted in 1785 by Nicholas Pocock when Bristol was Britain's most important port after London. The view is taken from Wapping Dock, site of the present M Shed museum.

The south-east prospect of the city by Samuel Buck, 1734. Prominent in the Temple area are the conical glass-making kilns which produced some of the goods bartered for African slaves. The lady on the right can be seen handing her child to a Negro servant boy.

of the middle passage were sold on arrival in exchange for colonial produce.

From that point the enslaved Africans belonged to the plantation owner and like any other possession had no rights. The use of African slaves was fundamental to growing the colonial cash crops. To maximise production, plantation overseers maintained a regime of fear with vicious and pitiless punishments.

The last leg of the slave ship's voyage was the passage home to England. The vessel was now loaded with raw sugar and other produce including cocoa, molasses, coffee, cotton,

An illustration of the 'Triangular Trade' which brought great wealth to some of the city's merchants, ship-builders, manufac-turers and bankers.

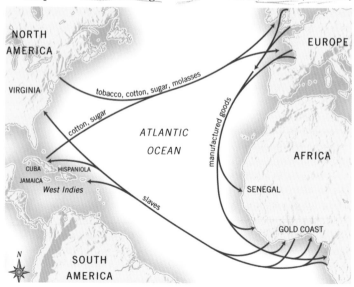

indigo, rum from the Caribbean and hemp and tobacco from Virginia. Refining raw sugar became a major industry in Bristol. Profits from the sale of sugar were used to purchase manufactured goods, continuing the merciless mercantile cycle.

The widely circulated image of the densely packed slave ship *Brookes*, became an understandably powerful force for the abolitionist campaign.

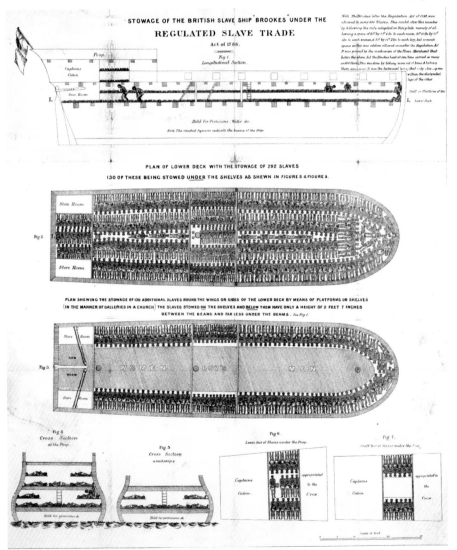

THE TRAILS

This book presents the story of Bristol's involvement in the slave trade through six discovery trails. The first four focus on the harbourside and bustling hub of the city. The concluding two walks explore the leafier, fresher areas of Clifton and the Avon Gorge in the steps of the wealthiest of the slave owners. Each trail reveals an aspect of the eighteenth-century city and features many of the personalities involved in the shameful trade and its eventual abolition.

Opposition to the slave trade was waged first by the Africans themselves, through a series of violent revolts, at sea and on land. In England, organised parliamentary opposition began in the 1780s but did not achieve success until 1807 when legislation abolished the trade in slaves but not slavery itself. A number of Bristol merchants who still had interests in Caribbean plantations resisted moves to emancipate their slaves. In the 1820s pressure to reform all aspects of English law and institutions gained momentum.

Parliament finally and formally legislated for the emancipation of enslaved peoples in British colonies in 1833, when the government agreed to pay compensation to plantation owners for their loss of slaves. British slave owners received a total of £20m (£16bn in today's money) from British tax payers. Full freedom was not actually granted until 1838, the year after Queen Victoria ascended to the throne.

This book has largely been made possible by the fact that one hundred and eighty years after abolition, British authorities are now disclosing the names and addresses of people whose fortunes were founded on slave ownership and the slave trade. No African has ever received any compensation.

TRAIL ONE

The walk begins at the 'M Shed' on Prince's Wharf. This 1950s' transit shed is now transformed into Bristol's History Museum.

The M Shed on Prince's Wharf is home to Bristol's History Museum.

1

M Shed – Museum of Bristol

M Shed is free to the public and presents the history of Bristol over 2000 years. Here one may discover the city's role in the transatlantic slave trade – who was involved, what was bought and sold, who stopped it, and what is the effect of the trade today?

On leaving the M Shed turn right and walk to the end of the building where there is a plaque which was unveiled in 1997 during the European Year Against Racism.

2

Quayside, Anti-Racism Plaque

This public acknowledgement of Bristol's role in the shameful trade was unveiled during the European Year Against Racism.

With the aid of displays, exhibits and state-of-the-art technology, the story of Bristol's role in the trans-atlantic slave trade is graphically presented and explained.

Bristol's public acknowledgement of the city's role in the shameful trade was unveiled in 1997 during the European Year Against Racism.

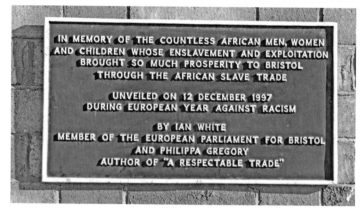

IN MEMORY OF THE COUNTLESS AFRICAN MEN, WOMEN AND CHILDREN WHOSE ENSLAVEMENT AND EXPLOITATION BROUGHT SO MUCH PROSPERITY TO BRISTOL THROUGH THE AFRICAN SLAVE TRADE

UNVEILED ON 12 DECEMBER 1997 DURING EUROPEAN YEAR AGAINST RACISM

BY IAN WHITE MEMBER OF THE EUROPEAN PARLIAMENT FOR BRISTOL AND PHILIPPA GREGORY AUTHOR OF "A RESPECTABLE TRADE"

Philippa Gregory, whose novel *A Respectable Trade* is set against the background of Bristol in the 1780s, is named on the plaque.

Using her vivid sense of history and inimitable storytelling skills, Philippa has illuminated this complex period of our past. Powerful, haunting, intensely disturbing, this is a novel of desire and shame, of individuals, of a society, and of a whole continent devastated by the greed of others.

Philippa was born in Africa but moved to Bristol with her family when she was two years old. She later attended Colston's Girls' School. This Academy is majority controlled by The Society of Merchant Venturers, whose trading links today are involved with defence contracting, tobacco, genetically modified crops and petroleum. The school was originally funded using the substantial bequest of Edward Colston, one of the richest and most successful of Bristol's slave traders.

Continue ahead and cross Wapping Road. Turn left then right to access Merchants Wharf.

3

Merchants Wharf

This modern housing development in the Wapping area of Bristol was built on the site of the shipyards of master ship-

This modern housing development stands on the site of Sydenham Teast's shipyard where slave ships were built and refitted.

wright Sydenham Teast. Teast was an investor in the slave trade who built a number of ships here specifically for that purpose and in 1786 refitted the slaving vessel *The Hector*.

In 1760, former sailor and artist Nicholas Pocock drew a sketch (shown below) of Teast's shipyard. A closer inspection of the original, held in Bristol's Museum & Art Gallery, reveals at least two figures of African or Afro-Caribbean origin, working as builders in the yard.

Nicholas Pocock's 1760 pen and ink wash sketch of Sydenham Teast's Wapping shipyard.

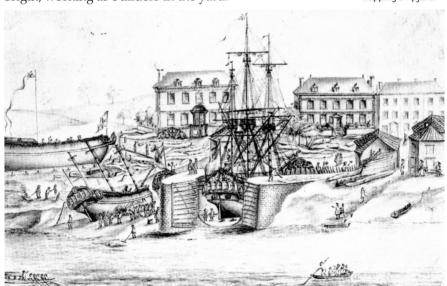

15

Continue along Merchants Wharf and turn right at Bathurst Basin. This was constructed in 1804-9 on the site of Trim Mills, two corn tide-mills owned by the Abbey of St Augustine, now Bristol Cathedral. Turn left over the footbridge to the Ostrich Pub.

4

Ostrich Pub

[handwritten annotations in left margin: Use Slave Trade ... site of ... it cut. + p...]

Dating from 1745 or earlier, the Ostrich Public House was used by sailors, shipyard and dock workers, merchants and others through the years when Bristol was a busy port.

A partly demolished wall in the bar reveals the interior of one of the many caves under the Red Cliff, formerly known as Addercliff. The caves were excavated to provide sand for glassmaking and ship's ballast.

The Ostrich Pub dating to 1775 or earlier, was extensively rebuilt after a fire in 1845.

Some of the internal decoration in the Ostrich has links to the slave trade including a copy of a pub trade card dated 1775

featuring a young black man, probably a slave. The pub today is popular
with locals and also attracts tourists
and visitors.

> *Leave the Ostrich and pass along*
> *Phoenix (formerly Alfred) Wharf*
> *then turn right to the entrance of*
> *Redcliffe Caves.*

5

Redcliffe Caves

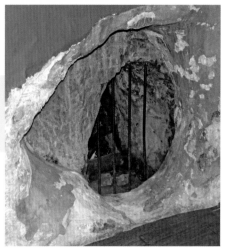

The plaque above the entrance to
Redcliffe Caves refers to the 'Middle
Passage' of the triangular slave voyages and wrongly implies
that slaves were incarcerated within the barred section. This
story may have originated because goods relating to the
African and West Indian trades were stored here. The only
other evidence linking the caves with the slave trade is an
eighteenth-century account of French sailors, some of whom
may have been black, being captured by Bristol privateers
during the Napoleonic Wars and held prisoner in the caverns.

This section of wall in the bar has been partly demolished revealing the interior of one of the many caverns under the Red Cliff.

The main product of the
caves was sand, needed
for the production of
glass for bottling beers
and spirits such as rum
(made from molasses
extracted from sugar
cane produced on slave
plantations) and other
glass objects including
'trade goods' for Africa.
On occasion Bristol City
Council opens the caves
for guided tours, but be
careful – it is easy to get
lost in the dark passages!

The entrance to Redcliffe Caves where sand was extracted for the production of glass bottles and other objects including 'trade goods' for Africa.

17

From the cave entrance head up the incline to the terrace of houses on Redcliffe Parade East.

Redcliffe Parade

These elegant brick built houses with stunning views across the docks were owned by wealthy merchants and others during the eighteenth century. One of the families living here was that of ship owner and merchant Thomas King who traded for palm oil, ivory and redwood, but was not a slave trader.

Many of the ships in King's fleet, including the *African Queen*, were built by Sydenham Teast, and the wealthy merchant was

These elegant eighteenth-century merchants' houses enjoyed stunning views across the docks.

able to observe their construction in the shipyards below his home.

Continue along Redcliffe Parade to the junction with Redcliffe Hill and turn left down towards the busy round-about.

The hospital of St John the Baptist was established in the tenth century for relief of the poor. It is thought to have been built on the site of the present roundabout. The hospital probably fell into disuse and ruin after the dissolution of religious houses during the reign of Henry VIII.

Until the 1960s shops and houses stood along this side of Redcliffe Hill. An area to the rear of these buildings known as Redrock Garden was purchased in 1665 by Quakers for use as a cemetery.

Turn left into the Quaker Burial Ground.

This peaceful little oasis near the busy Redcliffe Hill round-about continued in use as a Quaker burial ground until 1923.

7

Quaker Burial Ground

The Christian group, Quakers (The Religious Society of Friends) used this small plot of land as their burial ground for a number of years. Quakers generally believe in simplicity and their graves are usually marked by a simple stone, or have no marker at all.

By the eighteenth century some Bristol Quaker families had created very successful businesses and were wealthy traders and plantation owners, such as Charles and John Scandrett who were slave ship owners. Famous Quakers who benefited from the produce of slave labour included the Frys (cocoa), Lloyds and Barclays (banking and insurance for ships) and the Galtons (guns). Other families, less well known today but leading Bristol merchants of the period, included Champions, Goldneys and Harfords, whose brass and iron goods were traded to West Africa for slaves.

The Quakers were the first religious denomination on either side of the Atlantic to protest against slavery. By the 1760s Quakers decided that slavery was morally wrong and campaigned against the trade, many Quaker men and women becoming very active in campaigning for abolition. There were approximately 20,000 Quakers in Britain in the late eighteenth century, but they provided nine of the twelve members of the influential abolition committee that began meeting in 1787.

Against the back wall of the burial ground is the entrance to a fourteenth-century Hermit's Cave. John Sparkes, the first hermit, was installed here in 1346 by Thomas Lord Berkeley, to pray for him and his family. Successive hermits continued to occupy the cave until the seventeenth century.

Against the back wall of the burial ground is the fourteenth-century Hermit's Cave with 177 small Quaker headstones inside.

Inside the cave are 177 small Quaker headstones and several famous Bristol names are represented. The earliest is 1669, the latest 1923. The youngest was eight months, the eldest ninety-nine years.

Return to the roundabout and cross Redcliffe Hill to access St Mary Redcliffe church.

Members of the Society of Merchant Venturers who owned and invested in slave trade voyages contributed financially to St Mary Redcliffe church. Many of the Venturers were baptised, confirmed, married and buried here.

8

St Mary Redcliffe Church

The fine and impressive St Mary Redcliffe church is a good example of how a church can be enlarged and supported by a very wealthy congregation. Some members of the Society of Merchant Venturers, a group of rich Bristol merchants who owned and invested in trade businesses, including slave voyages and other activities related to the slave trade, gave money to the church. Many of the Venturers were baptised, confirmed, married and buried here or in the nearby Bristol Cathedral.

Within this church and the Cathedral are a number of monuments to wealthy members of slave-ship and plantation-owning families. They saw no contradiction between being a Christian and enslaving human beings. There is no written evidence to support a local story that slaves were kept in the caves below the church before they were sold.

In 1771 when William Wilberforce's bill to ban the trade of slaves failed in Parliament, the bells of St Mary Redcliffe and other churches across the city were said to have been rung as part of the celebrations.

On leaving the church cross the road again and walk up Redcliffe Hill. After passing the Mercure Bristol Hotel on your right turn right into Guinea Street.

Guinea Street

Originally called the Victoria, The Golden Guinea pub was adapted and renamed to reflect the history of the street.

This street is named after the gold coin 'the guinea', which took its name from the West African gold coast. An elephant and castle symbol seen on some of these coins came from the badge of the Royal African Company, the only British company allowed to trade in Africa before 1698.

Several merchants and ships' officers lived in Guinea Street, including Captain Edmund Saunders, a Church Warden of St Mary Redcliffe from 1732-1739. Saunders, who was in charge of 20 slaving voyages, had a house built for him which was later divided into three separate dwellings,

In an attempt at gentrification, ostentatious facades were added to the houses by the resident nouveau riche merchants.

10, 11 and 12. Number 12 still has its fine, original staircase and stucco ceiling.

In 1759 Joseph Holbrook, another sea captain resident in the street advertised a reward in return for information leading to the capture of a runaway slave *'a negro man, named Thomas, a native of the island of Jamaica… 5' 6" high, speaks good English and wears a brown wig'*. A sugar house on the corner of Lower Guinea Street was set up in 1797, one of a number in this area.

Walk to the end of Guinea Street then turn right then left over the footbridge to retrace your steps along Merchant's Walk back to the M Shed.

The Golden Guinea coin was named after the West African (Guinea) coast where much of the gold was derived. These coins were minted in the United Kingdom between 1663 and 1814 and were originally worth 20 shillings, or one pound sterling, later varying in value until becoming established at 21 shillings. During the Great Recoinage of 1816, the sovereign replaced the guinea.

23

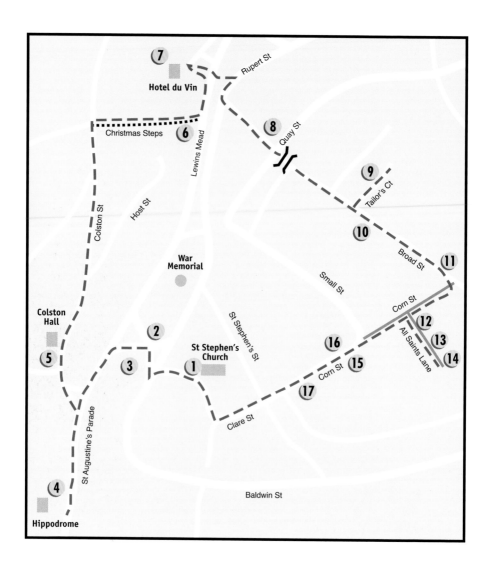

TRAIL TWO

The walk begins at St Stephen's church off Colston Avenue.

1

St Stephen's Church

History has given St Stephen's the dark, unenviable distinction of being the city's harbour church in the eighteenth century, when the slave trade flourished in the port. The site of St Stephen's was nothing more than marshland until the River Frome was diverted around 1247. Outside Bristol's west walls a harbour-side development grew with St Stephen's as its church.

St Stephen's was the harbour church for the city when the slave trade flourished in the port.

The church itself began as a cell of the Benedictine Abbey at Glastonbury and was first mentioned in 1304. St Stephen's survived as a parish church when Henry VIII dissolved Glastonbury Abbey.

Throughout the seventeenth and eighteenth centuries mercantile wealth enriched St Stephen's. This is confirmed by the amounts paid to clergy for sermons on Venturers' Charter Day. During the slavery era St Stephen's registered the largest number of African parishioners in Bristol's parish church records, partly due to its harbour-side location.

Ships' captains and officers would often return with an African servant as a capital gain on their investment. A list from parish records, shown as part of a display in the church, has the English names of 15 Africans baptised at St Stephen's before 1771, after which the legality of slavery in England was disputed.

Economist and political writer Josiah Tucker was curate and rector of St Stephen's for twenty-one years from 1737 before becoming Dean of Gloucester in 1758. He is best known for his writings advocating a free market and religious tolerance. While Dean of Gloucester he helped the abolitionist Thomas Clarkson with his early investigations into the slave trade. Tucker was a member of Bristol's first abolition committee in 1788 and friend of Rev. John Newton, the repentant slave captain who wrote the hymn *Amazing Grace*.

Part of a display in St Stephen's church listing the English names of 15 Africans baptised here before 1771, after which the legality of slavery in England was disputed.

Katherine Griseor, a Negroe (baptised 16 July 1715)
Thos. Smith, a Negroe (baptised 11 May 1721)
Daniel Steward, a Negroe abt. 20 Years old (baptised 22 April 1743)
Mary Milward, Mullatta, 28 Years old (baptised 18 April 1744)
Joseph Cornwall, a negro, adult (baptised 12 October 1744)
Elizabeth Beckford, a Negro Woman (baptised 6 August 1750)
Catherine, an Adult Black about 25 Years old (baptised 22 October 1753)
Joshua, another Adult Black (baptised 22 October 1753)
Mary, an adult Black (baptised 9 November 1753)
Jane Rodman, an Adult Black (baptised 28 October 1760)
Charles Welsh, an Adult Black (baptised 6 August 1761)
William Bristow, an Adult Black (baptised 22 January 1762)
John Milford, an Adult Black (baptised 14 March 1762)
Adam Game, a Negroe Man (baptised 14 September 1765)
George Harry, a Negroe Man (baptised 1 November 1765)

St Stephen's is the venue for 'Colston's Day', a joint annual service held on the birthday of Edward Colston (13 November or nearest weekday) by the Bristol Schools and Charities founded in his name. Colston was a prominent sugar merchant with interests in the Caribbean island of St Kitts. From his huge profits he contributed to many of the city's educational institutions, hospitals and housing, as well as restoring a number of churches.

From the Church take St Stephen's Avenue to the junction with Colston Avenue opposite Colston Tower. Cross both lanes of the highway via the pedestrian crossing to the green traffic island where you will see Edward Colston's statue on the right.

2

Edward Colston's Statue

The statue of Edward Colston, idealises him as a respected and charitable Bristol merchant but is silent about his role as a member of the Court of Assistants to the Royal African Company, which had the official monopoly over the slave trade until 1698.

Colston's relationship with the city remains a controversial topic of debate. Some Bristol citizens believe his statue should be removed and Colston Hall renamed in memory of enslaved Africans and in respect for their descendants.

Four Bristol charities established in the eighteenth-century in memory of Edward Colston still exist: The Colston Society, The Dolphin Society (1749), The Grateful Society (1758) and the Anchor Society (1769).

The controversial statue of Edward Colston, which some Bristolians believe should be removed, has stood in Bristol Centre for more than a century.

27

> *Continue south through the garden area to the statue of Edmund Burke.*

3

Edmund Burke's Statue

Burke was a statesman and Member of Parliament for Bristol. Throughout his political life he fought against injustice, cruelty and oppression, his attitude towards abolition however was at times ambiguous.

He campaigned for the trade's gradual abolition and produced a plan for ending it. Among his writings a *Sketch of a Negro Code* had a strange history. It was a detailed plan for the regulation of both the African slave trade and West Indian slavery. Never introduced in Parliament, it was seen by few during his lifetime and published fifteen years after his death.

Burke's attitude toward slavery remains a puzzle and begs the questions: What led him so early as 1780 to construct a detailed plan of regulation when the subject had not yet come under Parliamentary discussion, and why did he then set the project aside?

The statue of Edmund Burke whose attitude toward slavery remains a puzzle and continues to beg questions.

When the campaign to end the slave trade began in 1788 he spoke strongly in favour of its immediate ending. By 1792, however, he appeared to be co-operating with Henry Dundas, Home Secretary in William Pitt the Younger's government, who successfully side-stepped abolition during that year.

It was typical of Burke not to change even so evil an institution as slavery suddenly and drastically, but only prudently and through planned stages. However it was also typical that he recognized the evil as such and proposed to rid the British Empire of it.

Continue in the same direction until you are standing opposite the Hippodrome. Cross at the pedestrian crossing to the Drawbridge Pub.

Drawbridge Pub

Until very recently this pub on St Augustine's Parade was called the Horn and Trumpet. On its front is a smaller version of a Native American figurehead originally fixed to the prow of a Victorian paddle steamer, the *Demerara* which became stranded in the River Avon in 1851.

The figure is a romantic personification of Demerara, the former British sugar colony, now present day Guyana.

The boat's original figure was mounted on a building in Quay Street until it disintegrated during the building's demolition in the 1930s. The figure symbolises Demerara, the British owned sugar producing colony, now Guyana. In 1823, Demerara, was the scene of a bloody revolt involving almost all of the island's 12,000 plantation slaves.

A contemporary newspaper illustration of the retreat of Lieutenant Brady during the 1823 native revolt on Demerara, involving almost all of the island's 12,000 plantation slaves.

Turn right in front of the pub towards Colston Tower and bear left into Colston Street to arrive at Colston Hall.

Colston Hall

Colston Hall was built in 1867 on the site of Sir John Young's Great Tudor House. In 1653 it was converted into Bristol's first 'sugar house' refining sugar from the Caribbean. In 1708 the sugar warehouses were converted into Colston's Hospital which later became Colston's Boys School.

Since then, due to damage by fire and German bombing raids in World War II, the site has been occupied by four buildings named Colston Hall. The present one was opened in 1951 to mark the Festival of Britain. Campaigners, many from the city's Afro-Caribbean community, have called for the hall's name to be changed because of its continued association with the slave trade.

Continue up Colston Street passing John Foster's Alms Houses on the right to arrive at the top of Christmas Steps.

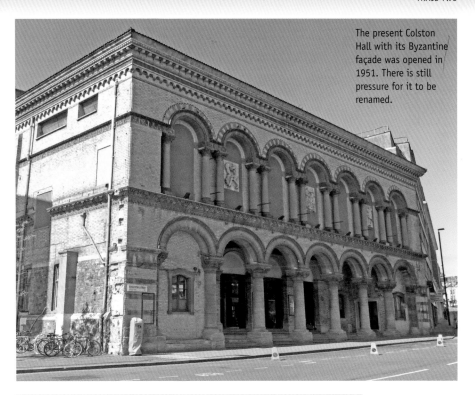

The present Colston Hall with its Byzantine façade was opened in 1951. There is still pressure for it to be renamed.

Descend the steps to the Christmas Steps Pub at the bottom on the right.

Christmas Steps Pub

Until spring 2015 this pub was named *The Three Sugar Loaves*, after a nearby sugar processing house, destroyed by fire in 1859. Sugar is highly combustible and fire was a constant hazard in the refining industry, destroying no fewer than 11 of Bristol's sugar houses between 1670 and 1859.

The high insurance costs prompted sugar merchants to start their own insurance companies, the first being Bristol Fire Office, founded in 1718. By 1837 this was absorbed into the

Until the second half of the seventeenth century the unique old town thoroughfare of Christmas Steps was a steep narrow alley described as being a breakneck and precipitous footpath, very perilous to passengers, especially in wintry weather and on dark nights.

Sun Fire Office, the only fire service in the city until 1877 when the Police Fire Brigade Service was formed.

Turn left up Lewins Mead to the Hotel du Vin.

Christmas Steps pub was formerly known as The Three Sugar Loaves.

Above: The beams and stripped brick walls of the basic interior evoke a sense of history.

Lewins Mead Sugar House

Lewins Mead Sugar House in Narrow Lewins Mead, owned by James Hilhouse, patriarch of Bristol's famous shipbuilding dynasty, is the only remaining example of the once thriving industry. Originally used to store and process sugar imported from the Caribbean, it has been preserved and converted into the Hotel du Vin. The first sugar house here was built in 1728 when Bristol was England's second city and when the River

Hotel du Vin was once a Lewins Mead sugar house used to store and process imported raw sugar from the Caribbean.

Frome flowed through the present City Centre. The view from the sugar house would have been a forest of tall ships' masts.

In the seventeenth century sugar was a luxury item but in the late eighteenth century was enjoyed by an increasing number of people to sweeten tea and cocoa. It was also used in the production of rum. Bristol was specialising in sugar processing and by 1760 the city had about 20 refineries like the one in Lewins Mead and was importing just under 14,000 hogsheads of raw sugar each year. The increased demand for sugar was reflected in the increased demand for African slaves to work the plantations.

Many sugar merchants owned large estates in and around Bristol. The Pope family, who owned one of the two sugar houses in Lewins Mead, began as grocers and soap makers before moving into the sugar trade and then becoming bankers.

The sugar house boiler room, complete with enormous chimney, is now the hotel reception and the former engine house a wine cellar.

In the late eighteenth century steam engines were developed to speed production and the refinery was re-designed accordingly. A boiler room (now the hotel reception), engine house, (now a wine cellar) and the chimney were added. The building finally ceased functioning as a refinery in 1831.

> *Leaving the hotel entrance cross Lewins Mead and Rupert Street to access Christmas Street ahead. Continue along Christmas Street crossing the road and passing under the archway of St John the Baptist church.*

8

Christmas Street and St John the Baptist Church

St John the Baptist church is part of the very fabric of Bristol built into the city walls in the fourteenth century as a place for travellers to offer prayers before a journey. St John's is the only remaining example of the five twelfth-century churches built into the city walls, forming part of the defences and providing sanctuary.

Before the organised slave trade of the eighteenth-century there was already a black presence in Bristol. The first African to be recorded in the city was an unnamed gardener employed towards the end of the 1500s at the Great House on what is now

St John's is the only remaining example of the five original medieval churches built into the city walls as places for travellers to offer prayers before a journey.

the site of Colston Hall. It is likely there were several hundred black people in Bristol in the 1700s. Some free black people, such as seamen, servants, actors and soldiers also visited or lived in the city.

Katherine, a black woman, worked in the Horsehead Tavern in Christmas Street until her death in 1612. Records do not indicate whether she was a slave or a free woman; however, like most taverns the Horsehead was also a brothel, so Katherine's services may have extended beyond that of barmaid, cook or cleaner.

Continue along Broad Street and turn second left into Tailor's Court.

Katherine, a black woman, worked in Christmas Street's Horsehead Tavern until her death in 1612.

9

Broad Street – Tailor's Court

Throughout the city, entrances led off the main streets into small alleys, yards and courts. Although many have since been built over, a few like Tailor's Court survive. To the right at the end of the court is Court House where William Miller lived. He was a grocer (meaning merchant), banker and founder member of the Company of Merchants Trading to Africa. In 1781 he died leaving £190,000 making him a multi-millionaire by today's standards.

The Guild of Merchant Tailors was one of the ancient guilds of Bristol, set up by charter of Richard II in 1399. It later

The Tailor's Guild building stands on the left hand side of the narrow court.

became a chartered company. The Tailor's Guild building on the left of the narrow court, was erected in 1740, replacing an earlier one on the same site.

The Guild's magnificent coat of arms decorates the porch hood and is contemporary with the building, but was restored in 1960. The moulding includes St John the Baptist's head on a platter. St John was patron saint of the Guild whose motto is *Concord makes small things flourish.*

The Court House on the right at the end of Tailor's Court was home to merchant and banker William Miller who made a fortune trading with Africa.

> **Exit Tailor's Court and note the Guildhall across the road.**

10

Broad Street – Guildhall

The first open meeting in Bristol on the abolition of the slave trade occurred in 1788, in the medieval Guildhall (now demolished) in Broad Street. A petition was drawn up and signed by, amongst others, George Daubeny (Merchant Venturer and one time mayor) and John Prior Estlin, the radical minister of the Lewins Mead congregation who was friends with Samuel Taylor Coleridge and Robert Southey.

The present Guildhall building, on the site of the original, no longer functions as the Guildhall and there are plans to convert it into a luxury 5 Star Hotel.

In 1788 the former Guildhall on this site was the venue for the first open meeting in Bristol for the abolition of the slave trade.

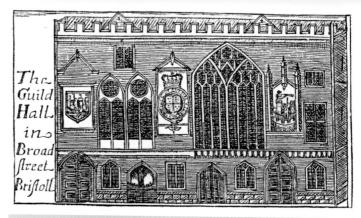

Continue along Broad Street to the junction with Corn Street and Cottle's Corner.

Cottle's Corner and Southey's Birth Place

At the junction where Broad Street, High Street, Corn Street and Wine Street meet there is a plaque on a building diagonally across from Christ Church marking the spot where Joseph Cottle, bookseller, publisher and poet had his business. Cottle was a fervent abolitionist who passionately criticised the slave trade. In his poem *Malvern Hills* (1798) he condemns:

> The Slave Merchants, Britons Blush to own!
> Who consecrate their influence, all their power.
> Not to improve, reform or elevate
> But to abase...

Abolitionists and dissenting writers in Cottle's circle included the 'clever young Quaker' Robert Lovell, son of a Bristol linen draper, Robert Southey and his brilliant friend Samuel Taylor Coleridge. In 1795 in an abolitionist lecture delivered by Coleridge he attacked 'the false and bastard sensibility by which men claim to be party to fine feelings whilst countenancing slavery.'

High on a building in Wine Street, attached to Christ Church, is another plaque informing us Robert Southey was born in a house near this site.

Southey, a devout Christian and England's Poet Laureate for nearly thirty-five years, wrote a dramatic poem called *Sonnet III* encouraging right thinking people to boycott sugar: '*Oh ye who at your ease Sip the blood-sweeten'd beverage!*' Referring to the blood of slaves who were brutally forced to work the sugar plantations.

The Sailor Who Had Served in the Slave Trade is one of Southey's most powerful images. It is based on a true incident in which a young Negro woman dies when a sailor is forced by a cruel captain to whip her because she refused to eat and tried to jump overboard.

Nets were put up round the decks of Guineamen to stop the valuable slaves committing suicide. Slaves who refused to eat were described as sulky and forcibly fed. For ever after, the sailor who whipped the Negress could get no peace of mind.

The site of Joseph Cottle's business where a red plaque informs us he was a bookseller, publisher and poet.

Devout Christian and passionate abolitionist, Robert Southey was England's Poet Laureate for nearly thirty-five years.

Southey's description of the mariner's torment we recognise today as post-traumatic stress disorder:

'I shut my eyes … it matters not,
Still, still the same I see,
And when I lie me down at night
'Tis always day with me!'

Head down Corn Street noting number 56 on your left.

12

56 Corn Street

Many goods were sold informally at coffee houses. In April 1758, local newspaper *Felix Farley's Bristol Journal* announced an auction to be held here for 100 hogsheads of white sugar and 70 casks of coffee, captured from a French ship in the Caribbean.

From the mid-eighteenth century, rewards for runaway slaves and the sale of slaves from the plantations were advertised in Bristol's newspapers, widely read in the city's coffee houses. On 12 January 1754 an advertisement in the *Bristol Intelligencer* announced: '*For sale* [to] *any gentleman or lady who wants a Negro Boy, a lad of 14 years recently landed* [from the Caribbean]'.

Turn left into All Saints' Lane with All Saints' Church immediately on your left.

13

All Saints' Church

Now an Anglican centre for religious education, this ancient church contains the tomb of Edward Colston who died in

56 Corn Street still trades as a coffee house and café.

1721. He was the son of merchant and sugar importer, William Colston, and in his early years lived in nearby Small Street.

In 1683 Edward Colston became a member of the Merchants Hall and was listed as a West India merchant who traded primarily in St Kitts. He was also a member of the London based Royal African Company which had the monopoly on the slave trade before it was opened up to Bristol and other ports. He amassed his fortune by owning a large fleet of ships, trading in sugar and was part-owner of a sugar house near St Peter's church in Castle Park.

Colston helped to fund the restoration of the tower at All Saints in 1716. It may be for this reason that a list of all his

All Saints' church where Colston is entombed is now an Anglican centre for religious education and can only be visited by appointment.

charitable bequests is inscribed on his tomb. There is no mention that between 1672 and 1689, his company transported around 100,000 slaves from West Africa to the West Indies and America including women and children as young as six, and that each slave was branded on their chest with RAC, the company's initials. To maximise profit, Colston's ships divided their hulls into holds with little headroom, in order to pack in as many slaves as possible.

Continue down All Saints' Lane towards St Nicholas Market with the Rummer Tavern ahead on the left.

Richard Jeffreys controversial painting 'The Death of Edward Colston' shows a kneeling African woman holding Colston's hand. She is thought by some to be 'black Mary', named as a servant in his will.

St Nicholas Market – Rummer Tavern

William Wordsworth, recalled in *Lines written a few miles above Tintern Abbey*: 'I began it upon leaving Tintern and concluded it just as I was entering Bristol'. It was finished in Joseph Cottle's parlour whose bookshop was around the corner from

The Rummer Tavern. The poem was published by Cottle as part of *The Lyrical Ballads*. Cottle was central to the support of Wordsworth, Coleridge and Southey during their West Country sojourn and Wordsworth's *The Prelude* 1805 contains these lines:

> *When to my native land,*
> *After a whole year's absence, I returned,*
> *I found the air yet busy with the stir*
> *Of a contention which had been raised up*
> *Against the traffickers in Negro blood…*

The Rummer Tavern was named after a large vessel for drinking rum.

Southey met Coleridge at Oxford in 1794 and filled his head with dreams of an American utopian community where self-ishness was to be extinguished, and virtue to reign supreme. The friends soon met again at Bristol and with Robert Lovell developed their 'Pantisocracy' idea – often discussing emigration plans over drinks at the Rummer.

Finance was the problem and Coleridge devised a fund raising idea of publishing a magazine to be called *The Watchman*. He convened his friends to a meeting at the Rummer, to determine the size, price, and frequency 'with all other preliminaries, essential to launching this first-rate vessel on the mighty deep'. Unfortunately, after only ten issues, the vessel sank and the long-suffering Cottle, once again stepped in to save the impecunious poet from debtors' prison.

The old fireplace where the romantic poets sat discussing the potential for a fairer world is now preserved behind a Perspex screen in a passage way leading to the gent's toilet.

Only part of the original inn survives as a pub and restaurant in All Saints' Lane – a narrow passage leading from Corn Street to the heart of the old Flower Market. The main section, running the length of the market and fronting the high street has been closed off and boarded up since 1999.

The present inn has been known as the Rummer (a large drinking vessel for rum) for over two hundred years but its history dates from 1241 when it was called the Greene Lattis and was granted Bristol's first licence. Today's interior has been stripped to clean simple lines but there are still some signs of antiquity to be found including the old fireplace around which the romantic poets sat in deep discussion.

Return to Corn Street turn left and continue to the Corn Exchange on your left.

15

The Corn Exchange

The present Corn Exchange was built in 1753 replacing the former building which had fewer grand facilities for Bristol's merchant class.

The present Corn Exchange was built in 1753 replacing the former building which had fewer grand facilities for Bristol's merchant class. Despite its name, it was intended for merchants of all types, and a number directly involved in West African and Caribbean trade used it for business transactions. However, it appears that most African and American merchants preferred to do business in the more informal atmosphere provided by nearby coffee houses.

Carvings on the front of the building are of African, Ameri-

Inside the main chamber, above three doors, are plasterwork emblems representing Asia, Africa and America. The female figure of America is wearing a headdress of tobacco leaves.

can, Asian and European figures and animals; symbols of Bristol's foreign trade. Inside the main chamber are emblems representing Asia, Africa, and America with the female figure of America wearing a headdress of tobacco leaves.

Continue down Corn Street.

16

Commercial Rooms

The Commercial Rooms, 43 to 45 Corn Street built in 1810 (three years after the end of the slave trade) as a new centre for Bristol's businessmen is now a Wetherspoon's pub.

The Commercial Rooms, 43 to 45 Corn Street, is now a Wetherspoon's pub.

The site was formerly occupied by Foster's Coffee House, another of Bristol's famous meeting places. Sometimes referred to as the three 'commercial' graces, the statues and carvings on the exterior of the building represent Bristol, Commerce and Navigation. One depicts Britannia checking the monies due to her from the rest of the world.

A little further down Corn Street note the NatWest Bank on the left.

17

NatWest Bank

A plaque on the wall of the NatWest Bank in Corn Street commemorates The Old Bank, originally set up in 1750 in

nearby Broad Street. This eventually, together with others, merged into the National Westminster Bank.

In the late eighteenth-century The Old Bank moved to the 'Wig and Pen', a pub at 35 Corn Street (now gone). All but one of the original founders were Merchant Traders to Africa, including Merchant Venturer Isaac Elton.

Elton was a dissenter of humble origin, the son of a market gardener who became one of the greatest commercial magnates of Bristol. He was an Alderman in 1699, Sheriff in 1702-3, Treasurer of the Merchant Venturers in 1705-8, Master in 1708-9 and Mayor in 1710-11.

A pioneer of Bristol's brass and iron foundries, Elton was also owner of its principal weaving industry and glass and pottery works, as well as having a large involvement in shipping.

Buying Clevedon Court in 1709 and Whitestaunton Manor in 1714, he was created a baronet in 1717 in reward for his services in the rebellion of 1715. He sat as a Whig for his native city from 1722 to 1727, when he stood down in favour of his son. Isaac Elton died on 9 Feb. 1728, leaving a fortune estimated at £100,000, perfectly demonstrating the connection between Bristol's slave trade and the development of the banking system.

Continue down Corn Street turn right into St Stephen's Avenue and left into the churchyard to arrive back at St Stephen's church.

Left: A plaque on the wall of the National Westminster Bank in Corn Street commemorates 'The Old Bank', originally set up in 1750 in nearby Broad Street. This was one of the banks, established with slave trade money that eventually merged into the National Westminster Bank.

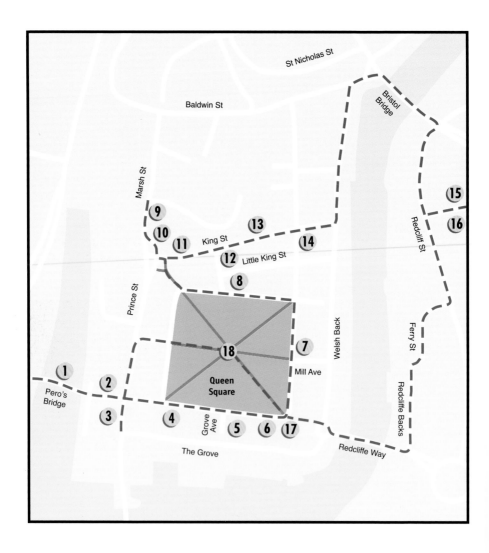

TRAIL THREE

The walk begins at Pero's Bridge.

1

Pero's Bridge

In March 1999, a new footbridge across the River Frome in Bristol harbour was named after Pero, a slave who lived and died in the city. In 1765, Pero Jones aged twelve and his young sisters Nancy and Sheeba were bought for the Mountravers Plantation in Nevis. Bristol plantation owner John Pinney paid £115 (about £5,750 in today's terms) for the three plus an adult slave.

Eighteen years later, when Pero was thirty he and another house servant, the freed slave Frances Coker, accompanied the Pinney family in their move back to England. Pero was

In March 1999, this distinctive foot-bridge across the River Frome in Bristol harbour was named after Pero who was brought to Bristol from the Caribbean island of Nevis as personal servant to planta-tion owner John Pinney.

A scene like this would have greeted Pero on his arrival at Bristol in 1783.

The waterside scene today from the eastern side of Pero's Bridge.

personal servant to John Pinney and Frances was lady's-maid to Pinney's wife Jane. Both 'servants' accompanied their owners on a visit to Nevis in 1790 and Pero went again in 1794. After this second visit, according to Pinney, Pero seemed to change. He started to drink heavily and his behaviour became unacceptable.

Pero fell ill in 1798 and his master decided a change of air would be beneficial and sent him to Ashton, outside Bristol where Pinney and his family often visited him. Pero was about forty-five and had served the Pinneys for thirty-two years. As far as we know, he was never given his freedom. He lived and died a slave.

Walk straight ahead into Farr's Lane to the junction with Prince Street.

Farr's Lane

This short street is named after Richard Farr whose family of ropemakers and slave traders prospered sufficiently to acquire Blaise Castle Estate. The slave ship *Prince of Orange* was owned by Richard Farr & Co. of Bristol. In 1736, on the second of four slaving voyages, the captain was Japhet Bird who kept detailed records and the following information is based on entries in his log book.

On the coast of West Africa, at least 273 slaves were bought and survived the voyage across the Atlantic to be sold in the Caribbean. Some of the enslaved Africans preferred death to whatever awaited them at the end of their voyage. 100 of the African men jumped overboard near the island of St Kitts and 33 of them drowned: '… more of them were taken up almost drowned, some of them died since, but not the owners loss, they being sold before any discovery was made of the injury the salt water had done them'.

At the end of this short road turn right into Prince Street and walk down to the Shakespeare Tavern on the right.

55

3

Prince Street and Shakespeare Tavern

In the eighteenth century Prince Street was a busy commercial and residential road but little of historic interest remains. The street is named after Prince George of Denmark, consort of Queen Anne, in whose honour Queen Square is named.

At the southern end, on the western side is the Shakespeare Tavern. The Shakespeare forms part of a terrace, designed in 1702 by architect John Strachan as houses for three Bristol

In the eighteenth century Prince Street was a busy commercial and residential road but little of historic interest remains. Mariner turned marine artist Nicholas Pocock, lived with his family at number 41 Prince Street (just beyond the barrels in the foreground).

merchants. Two of them, Combe and Becher, invested in slaving ships, as did other early inhabitants of Prince Street such as Henry Tonge and Thomas Coster, MP for Bristol for five years from 1734.

In Bristol Cathedral there is a monument to Thomas Coster who inherited the Upper Redbrook copper works from John Coster, his Bristol industrialist father. Thomas was part-owner of the *Amorretta* which shipped 178 Africans (including 34 children) from Angola to South Carolina in 1736.

The Shakespeare eventually became a dockside tavern in 1777 supplying refreshment for ship workers and warehousemen. Across from the tavern is The Grove, where waterside warehouses stored goods for ships plying the West African coast and the Americas.

Towards the far end of the street stood the Assembly Rooms, (marked by Assembly Rooms Lane) where merchants and

On the left of Prince Street, towards the far end, is Assembly Rooms Lane, the site of the Assembly Rooms, where merchants and their ladies danced the minuet at 6.30pm and less demanding country dancing at 8.00pm.

At the southern end of Prince Street is the Shakespeare Tavern, in the centre of a terrace of houses designed in 1702 for slave owners.

their ladies could dance the etiquette-laden minuet at 6.30pm and less skilled dancers could join in the country dancing at 8.00pm.

> *Walk back to the cross roads and turn right to access the southern side of Queen Square and the first American Consulate.*

4

Queen Square – The American Consulate

Queen Square was completed in 1727 when Bristol's involvement with the slave trade was nearing its height.

Queen Square was completed in 1727 when Bristol's involvement with the slave trade was nearing its height. The square is an indication of the kind of lifestyle enjoyed by Bristol's merchants and officials, made possible by wealth from the trade with Africa and the Caribbean in slaves and slave-produced goods. Like minuet dancing, this fine Georgian square is a reminder of the genteel lives Bristol's merchants and officials enjoyed, in contrast to the misery they inflicted on their slaves.

In 1775 seven merchants who traded with Africa, one who engaged in the West Indian trade, and a firm of tobacco merchants from Virginia, all lived in the square. By the early nineteenth century many merchants had left the Square escaping the bad odours and flooding of the harbour area. They built mansions in the fresher air of Clifton, on the hill above the industrialised port.

Only a very few of the original Queen Square buildings can still be seen today. The north side and much of the west was destroyed in the Bristol Riots of 1831 and later damaged by bombing in the Second World War.

This building stands on the site of the first American Consulate in Britain, established in 1792.

IN A HOUSE ON THIS SITE THE FIRST AMERICAN CONSULATE IN GREAT BRITAIN WAS ESTABLISHED IN SEPTEMBER 1792

Following the declaration of independence, slave-produced tobacco from the southern states continued to be important for Bristol's economy.

In 1792 the first American Consulate in Britain, was established on the south side of Queen Square. Trade with Africa, the Caribbean and America accounted for over half of

Bristol's mercantile business during the eighteenth century. Between 1698 and 1807 about 2100 slaving voyages sailed from Bristol.

Following America's declaration of independence from British rule on 4 July 1776, Bristol continued to trade with both the northern states of America and the southern slave states – hence the establishment of a consulate in Bristol representing American interests in the city. Slave-produced tobacco from the southern states was important to the city's economy.

Continue along the southern side of Queen Square across the junction with Grove Avenue to 33-35, the site of Woodes Rogers' house.

33-35 Queen Square

On 33-35 Queen Square a plaque commemorates Captain Woodes Rogers, who was an early resident of the square. He was Bristol's most famous privateer; one of a group of adventurous mariners who captained privately owned ships that had been approved by the government to engage in armed conflict.

Woodes Rogers's father built a successful long-distance shipping business, trading for fish in Newfoundland and, later, slaves in West Africa.

Celebrated for his voyage around the world from 1708 to 1711, Woodes Rogers junior made investments including the slave ship *Whetstone Galley*, which in 1708 took 270 African slaves to Jamaica. As a privateer, fighting against Spain he helped to keep the Caribbean under British rule. In 1717, at his own suggestion, he was rewarded for his efforts and made governor of the Bahamas, where he ended his days.

Continue to number 29, the offices of English Heritage.

33–35 Queen Square stands on the site of the house where the famous circum-navigator and privateer Woodes Rogers lived.

WOODES ROGERS 1679-1732 Great Seaman, Circumnavigator, Colonial Governor Lived in a house on this site

During his circum-navigation voyage in 1709, Rogers put in to the little-known island of Juan Fernandez where he discovered stranded Scottish sailor Alexander Selkirk who became the inspiration for the classic novel, written by Rogers' friend, Daniel Defoe and published under the title *The Life and Strange Surpriz-ing Adventures of Robinson Crusoe*.

In this 1799 family portrait by William Hogarth, Woodes Rogers's son, William Whetstone Rogers, is presenting his father with a map of Nassau, the capital of New Providence Island, in the Bahamas. Hogarth painted Rogers in profile to conceal his disfigurement from a Spanish musket ball.

29 Queen Square was built in 1709 for Alderman Nathaniel Day and is the best preserved of the original buildings in the square.

6

English Heritage Regional Headquarters.

29 Queen Square was built in 1709 for Alderman Nathaniel Day, who became Bristol's Mayor in 1737 and petitioned against a proposed tax on slaves. By mid-century, the house was home to Henry Bright, also one time Mayor of Bristol and a prominent merchant and slave trader.

As a Member of Parliament Bright was very active in the defence of plantation owners' rights. He supported the West India planters and merchants' petition for lower duties on sugar and rum and petitioned against the tax on slaves pointing out the *'unparalleled'* distress of the *'colonial body'*, many of whom had been *'reduced to absolute penury'*, and argued that there was no chance of ameliorating the condition of slaves while the colonists felt unjustly treated.

The house retains its original forecourt with gates and railings, and internally the panelling and staircase have been preserved.

On his death in 1771, Bright somewhat surprisingly left *'an annuity of £10 per annum, chargeable on the house where I now dwell, to my black servant, Bristol'*. This lovely house, which is the best preserved in the square, is now the regional headquarters of English Heritage.

Walk to the corner of the square and turn north passing the junction with Mill Avenue to Queen Square House.

7

Queen Square House

In addition to Nathaniel Day and Henry Bright, at least seventeen other men with links to the slave trade lived in Queen Square at various times. Among them were George Weare Braikenridge, Christopher Claxton, and Isaac Hobhouse.

West Indian merchant George Weare Braikenridge lived here in the most impressive house in the square.

West Indian merchant George Weare Braikenridge lived in Queen Square House. He was born in Virginia, the son of George Braikenridge a planter and merchant in Hanover County, but sent to England at an early age. He inherited an estate in Nevis and the deeds included information about 45 acres of land bought from the Pinney family.

Christopher Claxton, another merchant of Queen Square was an activist campaigning for the continuation of slavery. During the 1831 riots over changes to the voting system, Claxton's black servant refused to join the rioters. He was said to have thrown some of them out of the window of his master's house.

Continue walking round the square to Customs House on the corner of King William Avenue.

Customs House

Bristol's Customs House was originally located on the Welsh Back but was moved in 1711 to a specially built house on this

The present Customs House was built after the 1831 riots.

site in Queen Square. The function of the Customs House was to oversee the trade of the busy port and collect duties and other revenues from ships arriving and leaving the city's harbour. A large part of monies collected would have come from ships involved in the Africa trade.

> **Continue to the north-west corner of the square and bear right to access King Street. Bear left then right to the corner of King Street and Marsh Street.**

The devastation inflicted on the north side of Queen Square in the riots.

9

Marsh Street

We have George Weare Braikenridge, plantation owner and Queen Square resident, to thank for the drawing of the *Fortunes of War* pub in Marsh Street. Braikenridge was a collector and antiquary commissioning many local artists to produce images of the city.

In the 1820s, Marsh Street was a rough area near the quayside. There are said to have been 37 public houses on this street alone that were known for music, dancing, rioting, drunkenness and profane swearing.

This drawing of the former Fortunes of War pub in Marsh Street is from the Braikenridge collection held in Bristol Museum.

Thomas Clarkson, the anti-slavery campaigner wrote in 1808 that Bristol slave ship captains obtained crews for their slave ships in the mainly Irish-owned public houses in the Marsh Street area. In the 1820s one such pub, *The Fortunes of War*, featured a figure of a sailor with a wooden leg, loading the gunpowder into a cannon. Opposite this pub was once the bonded sugar warehouse of Messrs Robert Bird and Son.

Retrace your steps to King Street passing the site of Venturers' House on the left.

10

25 King Street Site of Venturers' House

Merchants' Hall was the eighteenth-century headquarters of the Society of the Merchant Venturers of the City of Bristol. A modern office building, with an informative plaque on the left of the main entrance, now occupies the site.

The guild of Bristol Mariners founded in 1445 maintained a priest and twelve poor seamen and their chapel of St Clement stood on this site. In 1552 they obtained a Royal Charter establishing them as the Society of the Merchant Venturers of the City of Bristol, with exclusive control of foreign trade. In 1558, the disused chapel became the Hall of the Society.

The Merchant Venturers were a powerful lobby, responsible in the eighteenth century for ensuring Bristol had its share of the African trade and defending the trade on the grounds that the city's prosperity depended on it. The original Hall was destroyed in the Second World War, and the present Merchants' Hall is now in Clifton.

Continue down King Street passing the Merchants' Alms Houses on your left.

Merchants' Alms Houses

In 1696 the Bristol Society of Merchant Venturers built their almshouses here for sick and elderly sailors. Those on the slave ships to West Africa often went blind or fell ill from various fevers and it is likely that some of them may have lived here.

The almshouses were originally built around a quadrangle but bombing and road realignment have left only three sides remaining.

In 1696 the Bristol Society of Merchant Venturers built their almshouses here for sick and elderly sailors to see out their days.

The Arms of the Merchant Venturers is displayed on their King Street almshouses.

Ahead on the opposite side is the King William Ale House.

King William Ale House

King Street is one of the few remaining streets in Bristol with a number of buildings owing their existence to the wealth generated by the slave trade. Living here in 1775 were Henry Webb, captain of the slaver the *Nevis Planter*, and Robert Walls, surgeon on the *Guinea* slaver.

The King William Ale House takes its name from King William III whose fine equestrian statue graces the centre of the adjacent Queen Square. Bristol's Merchant Venturers regarded the King, who, had ascended the throne in 1688 following the glorious revolution, as '*our Great and Glorious Deliverer*'.

Dating from 1670 The King William Ale House was originally part of a row of three terraced houses.

Dating from 1670 the King William Ale House was originally part of a row of three terraced houses. The remaining two are

In the atmospheric dimly lit front bar is a large stone fireplace and individual booths.

occupied by a restaurant and a second public house, *The Naval Volunteers*. The King William retains an eighteenth-century shop front and the original seventeenth-century door frame.

There are two entrances to the pub, in King Street and in Little King Street. The dimly lit interior has a very traditional feel and in the front bar there is a large stone fireplace and individual booths.

Further down King Street on the left is the Theatre Royal.

Theatre Royal

England's oldest working theatre opened here in 1766. The original 50 financial backers, many of them members of the Society of Merchant Venturers, each gave £50 towards the building. Investors included the Farrs, Henry Bright and Michael Miller, all living in Queen Square and participating in the African trade.

Another financial investor, George Daubeny was Bristol's Mayor in 1786. He was a sugar refiner and glass manufacturer, who lobbied for an end to the slave trade, but changed his mind and in 1789 joined the opposing committee.

England's oldest working theatre opened in 1766 with financial backing from members of the Society of Merchant Venturers.

Continue along King Street over the junction with Queen Charlotte Street passing the Llandoger Trow on the right.

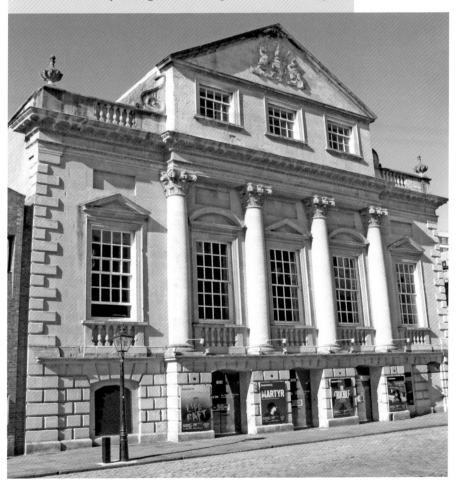

Tradition has it that the Llandoger Trow was the meeting place of Daniel Defoe and marooned sailor Alexander Selkirk, the author's inspiration for *Robinson Crusoe*.

14

Llandoger Trow

One of the most distinctive landmarks in King Street is the jettied façade of the ancient Llandoger Trow. The pub was partially destroyed by a bomb in World War II, but three of the original five projecting gables remain. A trow was a flat-bottomed barge, and Llandogo is a village 20 miles north-west of Bristol, across the Severn Estuary and upstream on the River Wye in South Wales. Trows were built here and sailed to trade with Bristol.

During his circumnavigation voyage in 1709, Captain Woodes Rogers put in to the little-known island of Juan Fernandez where he discovered stranded Scottish sailor Alexander Selkirk (see Queen Square). The pub promotes the tradition that Daniel Defoe met Alexander Selkirk, his inspiration for

Robinson Crusoe, here at the Llandoger Trow. Defoe was a friend of Woodes Rogers but unfortunately there is no evidence that the author and Selkirk ever met.

> *Turn left at the corner and walk up Welsh Back to the junction with Baldwin Street, then turn right over Bristol Bridge and bear right down Redcliff Street to the junction with Thomas Lane then turn left to St Thomas the Martyr church.*

15

St Thomas the Martyr Church

Originally the parish church to a thriving medieval trading area, St Thomas's was the finest Bristol church after St Mary Redcliffe. This handsome late eighteenth-century building was designed in 1789 by local architect and carver James Allen to replace the original medieval church by this time, deemed to be unsafe for use. The church still retains a beautiful eighteenth-century altar-screen, the only one surviving in the city.

Inside are a number of memorials to Bristolians engaged in the Africa trade, including John Harman Kater, a German from the Northern Rhine region of Westphalia. Kater, described as a 'Sugar Refiner', owned two houses in Tucker Street from which he left a bequest in his will to Sir Thomas White's Charity. Kater's memorial is unusual, crowned as it is by a *'sugar loaf'* and tools of his trade.

Another German with a family memorial in the church is Gunter Henry Kruger, planta-

Originally the parish church to a thriving medieval trading area, St Thomas's was the finest Bristol church after St Mary Redcliffe.

The memorial crowned by a sugar loaf, to John Harman Kater, his wife Mary and their two-year-old daughter Charlotte.

tion owner and sugar refiner. His plantation was in Martha Brae in Trelawny Parish on the north coast of Jamaica. Martha Brea had more sugar plantations than any other parish in the island and at one point had 27,827 slaves. Kruger lived at 15 Tucker Street near the Tucker Street Sugar House.

Across the narrow street is the Seven Stars pub.

16

Seven Stars Pub

The Seven Stars pub where, in late 1787, the Quaker anti-slavery campaigner Reverend Thomas Clarkson stayed, whilst investigating Bristol's involvement in the slave trade.

Little now survives of the old buildings in this parish, once home to rich clothiers, glovers, glassmakers, wine importers and sugar refiners whose trading activities supported St Thomas's church. One of the few remaining inns is the *Seven Stars* tavern, next to the church, where anti-slavery campaigner, Reverend Thomas Clarkson, gathered information on the slave trade.

In late 1787 the Quaker anti-slavery campaigner stayed at the *Seven Stars* pub while investigating Bristol's involvement in the slave trade. At great personal risk, Landlord Thompson guided Clarkson to the taverns of the old port and introduced him to a number of sailors who were willing to talk about conditions on board the slave ships. It was a very dangerous undertaking for Clarkson because most of the ship owners, merchants and investors felt it was none of his business. During his investigations around the country he was threatened and beaten up.

In addition to the inhuman treatment of the slaves, Clarkson also discovered the conditions for sailors on the ships were terrible. There was much bullying of sailors by officers, the danger of slave rebellions and a very high mortality rate.

Thirty-two crew members of the slave ship *Brothers* had died during a recent voyage. It was normal for up to a quarter of any crew and its prisoners to die from illness and disease during a round trip to Africa and the Caribbean. Though his name is not as well-known as William Wilberforce, Thomas Clarkson's evidence contributed significantly in bringing about the abolition of slavery in Britain.

This colourful relief plaque outside the pub tells the story of Clarkson's brave enterprise, helped by Mr Thompson, landlord of The Seven Stars.

From the Seven Stars retrace your steps to Redcliff Street and turn left, then turn right into Ferry Street and continue down Redcliffe Backs to Redcliffe Way, again turning right at the junction to cross the bridge. Continue straight ahead to the south east corner of Queen Square and the 'Hole in the Wall' pub.

Hole in the Wall Pub

The Hole in the Wall pub on the corner of Queen Square is a well known Bristol landmark. In the eighteenth century it was one of a number of taverns frequented by mariners who were constantly aware of the threat from press gangs. Sailors could legally be kidnapped during wartime and forcibly pressed into serving in the British Navy.

The spy house on the dock side of the pub was reputedly used as a lookout for press gangs as well as for government agents searching for smugglers. Although press gangs were not used to muster crews for slave ships, underhand methods were employed. It was common in many taverns around the centre

The spy house on the dock side of the Hole in the Wall pub was reputedly used to watch out for press gangs.

of Bristol for landlords to receive money from ship owners in return for getting sailors drunk by extending them credit and getting them into debt. The only way sailors could avoid debtors' prison was to sign up for a tour on a slave ship.

Head diagonally across Queen Square to the centre and the statue of King William III.

William III Statue

In the very centre of Queen Square is Michael Rysbrack's statue of King William III, an active supporter of the slave trade. This fine statue was largely funded by Bristol's Merchant Venturers, who considered William to be *'our Great and Glorious Deliverer'*. The Dutch prince had ascended to the throne in 1688 following the Glorious Revolution and replacing Catholic monarch James II.

Head west to leave the square via Middle Avenue to the junction with Prince Street to retrace your steps to Pero's Bridge.

Michael Rysbrack's statue of King William III largely funded by Bristol's Merchant Venturers.

The diagonal footpath across Queen Square.

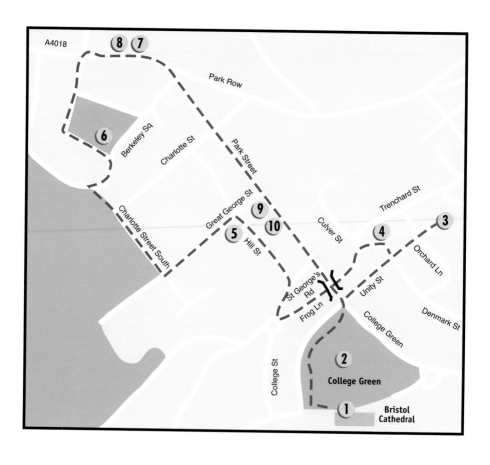

TRAIL FOUR

Start at Bristol Cathedral.

Bristol Cathedral

Located on College Green, Bristol Cathedral is one of the world's finest examples of a medieval 'hall church', with tall gothic windows and vaulted ceilings in the nave, choir, and aisles all at the same height. The main glory of the Cathedral is its east end, described by the famous architectural historian Nikolaus Pevsner as 'superior to anything else built in England and indeed in Europe at the same time'.

Located on College Green, Bristol Cathedral is one of the finest examples in the world of a medieval 'hall church'.

In the north transept is a late Victorian window honouring Bristol merchant Edward Colston who was linked with the London trading company controlling the early trade with Africa. The window is in recognition of the many charitable donations he made to the city from his slave trade businesses.

Edward Colston's memorial window in the north transept.

Along the very bottom a legend reads: 'TO THE GLORY OF GOD AND IN MEMORY OF EDWARD COLSTON 1636-1721'.

The successful merchant benefactor died in Mortlake and his body was carried back from London to Bristol. He is not interred in the Cathedral but in All Saints' church where his memorial lists all his charitable bequests.

On the walls of the Cathedral's north cloister are a number of memorials to parishioners who had connections to the West Indies. One significant monument is to the Daniel family of Barbados. Thomas Daniel, who was one of the biggest sugar

On the walls in the north cloister are memorials to parish-ioners who had connections to the West Indies.

merchants in the city, became so rich and powerful he was known as *'the King of Bristol'*.

There is also a monument to Thomas Coster, Member of Parliament for Bristol in 1734-9. He was part owner of the slave ship *Amoretta* which, in 1736, shipped 178 Africans (including 34 children) from Angola in West Africa to South Carolina in America.

The monument to Thomas Daniel and family of Barbados. One of the biggest sugar merchants in the city, Daniel became known as 'the King of Bristol'.

Among other interesting memorials is one to Mary Anne Schimmelpenninck (née Galton). Daughter of strict Quaker parents she became a significant writer against the slave trade and was one of the women who abstained from sugar as a protest against the enslavement of Africans. She wrote: '...both my cousins and I resolve to leave off sugar, as the only produce of slave labour within our province to discontinue'.

Curiously, on 29 September 1806 Mary Anne married Lambert Schimmelpen-

ninck of Berkeley Square, Bristol. He was descended from a branch of a noble Dutch family involved in the Bristol shipping trade. Lambert had commercial links with the Caribbean and was a partner in a firm investing in African slaves from Bristol.

A memorial plaque of particular interest today is that of Abraham Cumberbatch, the great-great-great-great-great-grandfather of actor and film star Benedict Cumberbatch. Slavery built the Cumberbatch fortune which, at its height in the mid-eighteenth century, made them one of Britain's wealthiest families, owning at least seven Barbados sugar plantations and a stately home near Taunton, in Somerset.

Their Cleland Plantation in Barbados was home to 250 slaves, who lived and died in conditions of unimaginable brutality. It was purchased in 1728 by Abraham Cumberbatch, and remained in the family until slavery was abolished in the 1830s, by which time it was owned by Benedict's great-great-great-grandfather, Abraham Parry Cumberbatch.

In an irony which even a Hollywood screenwriter couldn't invent, Benedict starred in the harrowing hit film *12 Years A*

Among other interesting memorials is one to Mary Anne Schimmelpenninck (née Galton) who became a significant writer against the slave trade.

Abraham Cumberbatch, from whom Benedict Cumberbatch is directly descended.

Slave, a true story depicting the ugly reality of the slave trade. He also appeared as William Pitt the Younger in the film *Amazing Grace,* about William Wilberforce recounting the experiences of John Newton, a crewman on a slave ship and his subsequent religious conversion.

From the Cathedral walk across College Green.

College Green

In 2013 the Bristol Records Office acquired a 270-year-old calf-skin-bound book of accounts which once belonged to Cran-field Becher, a prominent Merchant Venturer who lived at 12 College Green.

Becher's business log has revealed a chilling insight into the slave trade and attitudes to human trafficking including his written instructions to the commander of the *Jason Galley,* John Bartlett, ordering him to swap brandy and guns for *'as many Negroes as our ship can carry'.*

He specifies that the slaves should be *'not too old or decrepit'* and his entries make it clear that he views the unfortunate people as simple commodities to be bought and sold like the *'good quantity of elephants teeth'* he was also hoping to obtain. The enslaved people were transported to Carolina where they were sold for £18 each.

The accounts detail the costs of fitting out the ship, the provisions taken on board, the type and value of the cargo from Bristol to Africa (including cotton goods, brandy and guns), the return leg to Bristol loaded with rice, sugar and other goods, and the profits made by the merchants.

Captain Day was another resident of College Green. He had *'a Christian Negro'* servant called Richard Cornwall. In 1737, a local white woman named Cornwall as the father of her child and tried to prove this through the courts. He was acquitted apparently, when it was discovered the child named as his had been coloured with coal dust to make it appear black.

If Cornwall had been found to be the baby's father, he would have had to pay the mother for its upbringing. The relationship between the two is not known, or why the woman named him as the father.

James Hilhouse, patriarch of the hugely successful Bristol firm which built ships for the Africa trade, lived very modestly in a house on College Green until his death in 1754. Within a few years his wealthy and upwardly mobile son moved to Clifton to the impressive mansion of Cornwallis House *(see walk 5)*.

> *Walk across College Green to the junction of Park and Unity Streets. Continue down Orchard Street crossing the junction with Denmark Street and Orchard Avenue.*

3

Orchard Street

This lovely street with its elegant Georgian houses was first laid out in 1717. James McTaggart, captain of the slave ship

These elegant Georgian houses were home to a number of Huguenot refugees turned slave traders.

the *Africa*, lived here and it was also the location of the offices of Caribbean merchant, Mark Davies.

The present offices of Bristol Municipal Charities at number 14 stand on the site of a chapel built in the eighteenth century by Huguenots, refugees who left their homes in France to escape religious persecution. Ironically, at least two of the wealthier Huguenots, James Laroche and Louis Casamajor, became prominent slave traders and persecuted Africans.

Another Huguenot, Stephen Peloquin, became one of the five wealthiest men in Bristol in the eighteenth century. He built his fortune from the tobacco trade which depended largely on slave labour. Peloquin left his estate to his daughter Mary Ann, who was noted for her charitable donations. During her lifetime she lent her house in Queen Square to Josiah Tucker, a prominent anti-slavery campaigner.

> *Return up Orchard Street to Denmark Street and turn right to the Hatchet Inn in Frogmore Street.*

4

The Hatchet Inn

The Hatchet Inn in Frogmore Street (originally Frog Lane) is Bristol's oldest inn. Dating from 1606 or earlier it is thought to have been built on the site of a farm. Its unique name refers to the axes used for tree-felling by Clifton foresters. Frogmore Street today is a back water spanned by the elevated main thoroughfare of Park Street but had been of great importance as the chief way of driving from the city to the former village of Clifton before Park Street was built.

The Hatchet Inn in Frogmore Street, would have been a meeting place for business men engaged in the slave trade.

The inn would have been the scene of business meetings between merchants, plantation owners, bankers and government officials – in short, all who had a vested interest in the slave trade and the larger institution of slavery.

Walk down Frogmore Street passing under the road bridge to Frogmore Lane. At the mini-roundabout turn right into St George's Road and left into Hill Street. At the junction with Great George Street turn left and walk up to the Georgian House Museum.

5

The Georgian House Museum, Great George Street

The Georgian House at 7 Great George Street was built about 1790 by plantation owner John Pinney and is furnished today as a period townhouse. It presents a picture of what life was like for a wealthy businessman towards the end of the Georgian period (1714-1830).

7 Great George Street, now the Georgian House Museum.

Pinney owned plantations on the Caribbean island of Nevis and used slave labour to grow and harvest sugar cane. After settling in Bristol he employed managers to run his plantations and started a factoring company trading in sugar.

It was in 1765 that John Pinney first left England for the island of Nevis in the Eastern Caribbean. Seven years later, whilst on the island, he met and married Jane Weekes, the daughter of William Weekes, who gave himself the title of: *'Treasurer and Commander of all Forts and Fortifications and Plantations on Nevis'.*

Pinney saw no wrong in using slave labour on his holdings to grow and harvest sugar cane.

John Pinney, who owned plantations in the Caribbean island of Nevis, built 7 Great George Street around 1790.

The Pinneys had seven children, five being born on Nevis. Their son Charles was born on 29 April 1793, in what is now the Georgian House Museum. On 25 October 1832 Charles Pinney was put on trial in the court of King's Bench, charged with neglect of duty in his office as Mayor of Bristol during the riots *(see walk 5).*

John Pinney had a black manservant called Pero whom he brought from Nevis and who lived for some years in the

The study in the Georgian House Museum from where Pinney conducted his business which included the purchase and sale of slaves.

We do not know what Pinney's servant Pero looked like but he would have worn his master's livery and would therefore have been dressed like actor Ariyon Bakare, who played Mehuru in the 1998 TV mini series based on Philippa Gregory's novel *A Respectable Trade*. The drama also starred Emma Fielding and Warren Clarke.

Georgian House. A footbridge on Bristol's harbourside was named after him in 1999 *(see walk 3)*. It commemorates and pays tribute to all Africans and West Indians who were enslaved by Bristol's merchants and planters.

> *Continue along Great George Street and turn right into Charlotte Street South, then walk along the edge of Brandon Hill Park to exit into Upper Byron Place and keep right to Berkeley Square.*

6

Berkeley Square

Thomas Daniel, one of the wealthiest of Bristol's merchant princes, returned to Britain from Barbados in 1764 to live in Berkeley Square.

Much of the development in the area of Upper Park Street was begun in 1787 by members of the Paty (or Patty) family, the leading architects in Georgian Bristol. The Patys were responsible for many of the large, distinctive houses built for prosperous merchant families in Great George Street, Charlotte Street and Berkeley Square.

Thomas Daniel, one of the of the biggest sugar merchants and wealthiest of Bristol's merchant princes, returned to Britain from Barbados in 1764 with his wife Eleanor and son (also named Thomas) to live in Berkeley Square. He became so rich and powerful he was known as '*the King of Bristol*'. Records show that this already obscenely rich man owned 8970 slaves in 1833, and received a staggering £257,032 in compensation when they were freed, the equivalent of £22 million in today's money.

Thomas junior, who inherited the family business, became Mayor of Bristol in 1797 and chosen Alderman in 1798. He married Miss Cave, sister of Daniel Cave whose family had extensive interests in Caribbean slave plantations and became a partner in Ames, Cave & Co. Bankers and sugar merchants.

Near the bottom of the 'rich list', at 46 in the top 50 compensation payouts, was Henry Sealy, of 29 Berkeley Square. He received £391, only £33,560 at today's value.

29 Berkeley Square was home to Henry Sealy. A two bedroom flat in this house has just sold for £315,000.

Walk round the square to the junction with Park Street opposite the Wills Memorial Building.

The Wills Memorial Building

Dominating the street scene at the top of Park Street is the Wills Memorial Building. Dating from 1903 it was a gift to Bristol University from the Wills family who made their fortune in the tobacco trade, important to Bristol in the eighteenth century when slave-produced tobacco came largely from plantations in the American Republic.

The family was involved in a number of charitable activities in Bristol including subscribing to the 1793 edition of a book written by former slave Olaudah Equiano. In his autobiography, Olaudah writes that he was born in the Eboe province, in what is now southern Nigeria and describes how he was

The Wills Memorial Building, dating from 1903, was a gift from the Wills family to Bristol University.

STANSFIELD & COS
Super Fine Tobacco,
Castle Street BRISTOL

kidnapped with his sister at around the age of eleven, sold by local slave traders and shipped across the Atlantic to Barbados and then Virginia.

The book, first published in 1789 attracted wide attention and was considered highly influential in gaining passage of the Slave Trade Act of 1807, which ended the African trade for Britain and its colonies.

On this trade card the image of African slaves is used to promote tobacco. The shield of the Merchant Venturers Company is also included.

Next door to the Wills Memorial Building is the City Museum & Art Gallery.

8

City Museum & Art Gallery

Freed slave Olaudah Equiano whose highly influential autobiography helped to bring an end to slavery.

The Museum & Art Gallery was *'The gift of Sir William Henry Wills Bart, to his fellow citizens 1904'.* A major exhibition here in 1999 portrayed Bristol's role in the transatlantic slave trade. Presented as *A Respectable Trade*? it became one of the most visited exhibits in the history of the museum. Much of its material is now on display in the M Shed.

The Art Gallery houses a collection of paintings by Nicholas Pocock, son of a seaman, born in Bristol in 1740 who lived at 41 Prince Street. Nicholas followed his father's profession and was master of a merchant ship by the age of twenty-six. During his time at sea, he became a skilled artist, producing ink and wash sketches of ships and coastal scenes for his log books.

The first authoritatively-attributed drawings by Pocock date from 1758 and, apart from one evocative picture of Wapping

Nicholas Pocock ship's captain turned renowned maritime artist.

The City Museum & Art Gallery at the top of Park Street.

Pocock's 1760 painting, *The Southwell Frigate* shows a Bristol slave ship trading on the West African coast.

Docks *(see walk 1)*, are all of Bristol privateers and slave ships. His 1760 painting, *The Southwell Frigate* features a Bristol slave ship trading on the coast of West Africa. The central sections of the painting show views of the ship at sea while details to the left and right depict the crew unloading trade goods and the captain buying slaves from his African trading partner and supervising their loading.

Pocock's idealised depiction of Nevis, as seen from St Kitts, was commissioned by slave plantation owner John Pinney.

In 1778 Pocock's employer, Richard Champion, became financially insolvent due to the effects the American Revolutionary War had on transatlantic trade. As a consequence Pocock gave up the sea and devoted himself to painting. The first of his works was exhibited by the Royal Academy in 1782.

Pocock learned how to please his patrons. One of his later paintings was commissioned by slave owner John Pinney and depicts an idealised view from St Kitts of the island of Nevis where Pinney had his plantations. The characteristic features of the area are shown as Pinney wished to remember it and to show to friends. The day to day grind of work on the plantations is kept out of sight. The foreground with English oaks, cattle and country people might easily be an English pastoral scene.

From The City Museum & Art Gallery walk downhill forking right into Park Street to the junction with Great George Street.

9

Corner of George Street and Park Street

Nearby were the offices of Richard Farr, an Alderman (assistant to the Mayor) and slave trader. On the corner was the home of Henry Cruger, the New York born merchant, who became Mayor of Bristol in 1781 and later a Member of Parliament. Cruger married the daughter of banker Samuel Peach of Tockington. Peach was part-owner of the slave ships *Cape Coast* and *Kingston*, which in 1757 and 1759 respectively, sold a total of 631 Africans to American plantation owners.

Whilst an MP Cruger campaigned against the immediate end to the slave trade, arguing that were this to happen, it should be done on a gradual basis, and that all merchants should be compensated for the loss of earnings. He later returned to America and became a U.S. Senator. A plaque on the building commemorates Cruger's residence.

A few steps further down the hill, on the same side, is the site of number 43.

10

Site of 43 Park Street, Now Demolished

A little further down Park Street on the same side is number 43, the site of a school for young ladies established by Bristol Quaker, Hannah More, who was a leading campaigner for better education for the poor, taking part in Quaker actions against the slave trade. She was a friend of William Wilberforce and Thomas Clarkson, who were the forces behind the abolition campaign. Hannah More voiced her objections to the slave trade by openly criticising Christians who were involved. She stated that they are not Christians who infest Africa's shores, but are rather white savages ruled by lust for gold or lust for conquest.

Hannah More, friend of William Wilberforce and Thomas Clarkson, was a leading campaigner for better education for the poor and took part in Quaker actions against the slave trade.

Despite being unable to vote, Quaker women were very active campaigners and speakers about issues which con-

Henry Cruger born in America in 1739, became a resident of Bristol and lived in this house on the corner of Great George Street and Park Street from 1757 until 1790

cerned them. In 1778 Hannah More joined the large scale boycott of slave grown and harvested sugar which helped publicise the horrors of slavery. This was one of the first public political campaigns involving women.

A legacy of the slave trade manifested itself during World War II. Park Street was designated for white troops from the United States Army. On the evening of 15 July 1944, black soldiers entered the area and fighting broke out between about 400 GIs. 120 Military police broke up the fighting but one was stabbed. Several soldiers were shot and one died. The city was then placed under military curfew.

Continue down Park Street to return to College Green and the Cathedral.

Master of the Merchant Venturers Society 1781, New Yorker Henry Cruger, became Mayor of Bristol. He holds the unique distinction of having been a Member of Parliament and a U.S. Senator.

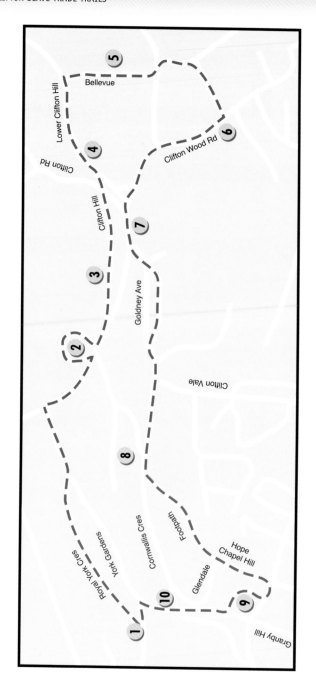

TRAIL FIVE

We begin our walk above the Avon Gorge at the foot of steps leading from Wellington Crescent up to Clifton's architectural showpiece, Royal York Crescent.

During the first half of the eighteenth century some of the more prosperous of Bristol's slave trading merchants moved out of the cramped houses and pollution of the old city. Taking advantage of the peace and clearer air they built luxurious individual mansions on Clifton's hills and funded the development of elegant terraces. Some of these buildings still survive such as Royal York Crescent, Saville Place, Clifton Court, Clifton Hill House, Bellevue, Clifton Wood House, Goldney House (now Nuffield Hospital) and Cornwallis House in Cornwallis Crescent.

Six Bristol merchants, most of whom had African or West Indian links, financed the first phase of building of Royal York Crescent.

1
Royal York Crescent

Royal York Crescent, reputed to be the longest terrace in Europe, is set majestically high on the hillside and visible from the gorge below and across the harbour. Today, most of the 46 Grade II listed houses are divided into leasehold flats which sell for an average of half a million pounds.

The Crescent, with its colourful wrought iron balconies, raised walkways and distinctly 'colonial' style was designed by William Paty. Construction began in 1791 but bankruptcy of the developer in 1793, resulting from the war with revolutionary France, brought work to a standstill.

In 1801 the Government bought the land and unfinished portion of the Crescent, intending to build barracks. Fortunately local opposition frustrated this plan and the crescent was completed in 1820 as originally envisaged.

Redwood Larwood who lived at 33 Royal York Crescent owned 230 slaves in Antigua.

The project was funded by six merchants – most having had African or West Indian links. They were John Cave, Joseph Harford, William Fry, William Gibbons, George Daubeny and Richard Vaughan. John Cave, Joseph Harford and George Daubeny were also among the founding partners of Bristol's first bank.

When Parliament finally abolished slavery in 1833 and granted £20 million in compensation, to be paid by British taxpayers to the former slave-owners, John Cave of Brentry House, Westbury-on-Trym received £1984 (£170,300).

Front doors of the houses open on to a raised pavement or

terraced walk with basements and vaults below. The designs vary slightly with different builders. Redwood Larwood, a plantation owner who had slaves in Antigua, lived at 33 Royal York Crescent. He received compensation of £3493 15s 9d for the loss of 230 slaves.

Walk the length of the raised pavement of Royal York Crescent turning right down Regent Street and left into Saville Place.

Saville Place

When Britain went to war with Revolutionary France in 1793 the building boom collapsed and developers and builders were ruined overnight. Hundreds of houses were left half built. A glance at Saville Place shows the 'before and after' effect.

A glance at Saville Place shows the 'before and after' effect of the financial collapse. The houses in the foreground are a cheaper Victorian extension of the original Georgian terrace.

97

The 1841 census shows that sixty-five year old Thomas Sealy was living at 4 Saville Place with wife Mehetabel (also sixty-five), daughters Margaret forty, Mary thirty five and son Rev. William Drake Sealy thirty all born in Barbados. In the compensation payouts Thomas Sealy received £5450 (£467,800) and his son Rev. William Drake Sealy was awarded £2180 (£187,100).

Continue east along Regent Street and fork left into Clifton Hill to arrive at Clifton Court on the left.

3

Clifton Court (Now Nuffield Private Hospital)

Clifton Court was home to wealthy brass merchant, Nehemiah Champion II, and his wife, Martha Goldney, daughter of Thomas Goldney II.

During the eighteenth century Bristol was the principal brass producing area in England and the industry was important to the city's commerce. The growth of the slave trade and development of the British brass industry were linked. Brass and copper trade goods were a significant part of the slave ship cargoes bound for Africa.

The Baptist Mills Brass Works started in 1702 by Abraham Darby were taken over in the 1720s by Quaker Nehemiah Champion. The company was known as the Bristol Brass & Copper Company and investors included members of the Goldney and Harford families. A stocktake in 1767 estimated the worth of the works and stock to be £300,000 (about £20 million today).

Clifton Court, built in 1742, was one of the first mansions in the area and was home to wealthy brass merchant, Nehemiah Champion II, and his wife, Martha Goldney, daughter of Thomas Goldney II. The impressive house is now a Nuffield state-of-the-art private hospital.

Continue east along Clifton Hill until it becomes Clifton Road and take a footpath on the right to reach Clifton Hill House.

4

Clifton Hill House, Lower Clifton Hill

Clifton Hill House was designed by Isaac Ware and built in 1747 for Paul Fisher, linen draper, merchant and ship owner. Fisher, son of an important Africa Merchant, was himself a member of the Company of Merchant Venturers trading to Africa. He also had financial interests in a Grenada plantation and the West Indies and Carolina trades.

The date 1747 above the entrance porch incorporating Paul and Mary Fisher's initials, was carved by mason Thomas Paty, later to become a famous Bristol architect. The property now belongs to Bristol University. Gardens at the rear slope away from the house and during the Fisher's residence ships in the harbour would have been clearly visible.

Continue east down Lower Clifton Hill and turn next right into Bellevue.

Clifton Hill House was designed by Isaac Ware and built in 1747 for Paul Fisher, linen draper, merchant and ship owner.

The terrace houses of Bellevue were built in the 1780s during Clifton's great building boom.

5

17 Bellevue

For a few years during the 1780s' building boom, most of the major terraces of Clifton were laid out. These include The Mall, Rodney Place, Richmond Terrace, Prince's Buildings, Cornwallis Crescent, Sion Hill and Bellevue.

A memorial to William Hepburn in Clifton parish church informs us he was *'of the Island of St Vincent'* and *'departed this life January 25th 1846'*. Hepburn, who lived at 17 Bellevue, had 79 slaves in the island of St Vincent. He counterclaimed before withdrawing as judgement creditor on Spring Estate and the compensation of £2003 14s 11d went to trustees including his daughter Harriet Hill. It seems likely it was this same William

An idealised view of slaves enjoying 'A Negro Festival' in the island of St Vincent.

Hepburn who was awarded compensation for six enslaved people in Castries, St Lucia.

Continue down Bellevue and turn left at the junction with Constitution Hill. Cross the road and take the cobbled footpath into Bellevue Crescent, turning right along Glenworth Road. Continue to the junction with Clifton Wood Road where Clifton Wood House comes into view.

6

Clifton Wood House, Clifton Wood Road

High security on the property means Clifton Wood House can now only be glimpsed from Clifton Wood Road.

Clifton Wood House dates from the 1720s and was acquired in 1747 by the Goldneys, a famous Bristol merchant dynasty. The Grade-II listed mansion remained in the family's estate for more than 200 years and was rented out to a number of wealthy merchants including slave trader Richard Farr.

The house changed hands in the nineteenth century and was used as a children's home before being purchased for use as

a hall of residence by Bristol University in the 1950s. In 2000 it was sold for £1.25 million to wealthy local businessman Petros Birakos, who converted it into a most impressive family home.

The property, now owned by the Royal Bank of Scotland, comprises luxury apartments with high security.

Bristol University used the house as a hall of residence for about fifty years from 1950.

Protected by electrically operated gates, it can only be glimpsed behind high walls and hedges.

Walk to the top of Clifton Wood Road and turn left into Goldney Avenue where Goldney Hall appears on the left – it is better appreciated from the elevated green opposite.

Goldney Hall

The Goldney family first lived in this house in 1694, when Thomas Goldney II rented it; purchasing it later in 1705. At that time the manor of Clifton largely belonged to the Society of Merchant Venturers.

During the 1720s it was rebuilt by Thomas Goldney II with garden features added, but most of what is seen today was the work of his son Thomas Goldney III and later the Fry family who were its nineteenth-century owners.

The first Thomas Goldney, born in 1620, was an active Quaker and a successful grocer. It was his son, Thomas Goldney II, who was a partner in the Warmley Brass Works outside Bristol, and went on to develop ironworks in partnership with Abraham Darby in Coalbrookdale, Ironbridge, Shropshire – which played a key part in the British industrial revolution.

Thomas Goldney II, purchased Goldney Hall in 1705.

Goldney II also invested in shipping, and in 1708 was one of the main backers of the epic voyages of two ships, *The Duke*

and *The Duchess*, led by Captain Woodes Rogers. These expeditions, involved the capture of Spanish ships, such as the legendary *Manila* galleon, and raids on South American ports.

The Goldney family first rented this house in 1694.

Some of the vessels Woodes encountered and raided would have been slavers, whose human cargo he would have captured and sold. The Goldneys were therefore involved indirectly in establishing British industrialization, partly from the gains of the slave trade. Later as participants in the prominent Quaker network at the centre of the growing movement for Abolition, the Goldney family was also associated to some extent with its end. Goldney Hall, is now one of Bristol University's halls of residence.

Keep to the left and continue west to the junction with Cornwallis Crescent.

Cornwallis House

Well-connected Bristol ship builder James Martin Hilhouse constructed marine craft including stout wooden merchantmen up to Navy warships. Over two centuries his business

Cornwallis House, built by Bristol's most successful shipbuilder, James Martin Hilhouse, is now divided into apartments.

and the subsequent 'Hilhouse & Hill' run by his son, were the most important shipbuilding enterprises in Bristol's long maritime history. The two companies built and launched over 560 ships.

James Martin's grandfather (also called James) was an enterprising Glaswegian who had moved south in the eighteenth century to seek his fortune. He became a successful Bristol

Part of Cornwallis House gardens.

sugar merchant, married well and lost little time in joining the Society of Presbyterian Dissenters, based at Lewins Mead Chapel. He became a member (and later Master) of the prestigious Society of Merchant Venturers.

By 1728 James had his own sugar refining house in Lewins Mead which is now the Hotel du Vin *(see walk 2)*. Ships in which he had shares left Bristol docks for the West Indies, especially Jamaica, with stores and supplies for the plantations returning home loaded with barrels of raw sugar for refining in Bristol.

Unlike many other Bristol merchants, such as the Pinneys or the Brights, the family did not own West Indian plantations or slaves. They reasoned greater money was to be made from kitting out privateering ships, 'letter of marque' vessels which carried a legal, Government-backed licence for a little discreet 'piracy' on the high seas.

James, who lived very modestly, died in 1754 and within a few years his wealthy and enterprising son built Cornwallis House, moving there from the old family seat in College Green. Only a few years later James junior, who like his father and grandfather before him had been a councillor and sheriff, was dead at the age of forty-three.

His son and heir, James Martin, saw his future in building large ships for the Navy. However, his very first vessel off the stocks in 1776 was the *Exeter*, a 300-ton merchantman built for the Jamaican sugar trade.

James Martin Hilhouse had artistic ability and befriended many Bristol artists, including the much-talented Nicholas Pocock whom he commissioned to paint a number of his vessels including the *Cleopatra* in 1779.

A pen and wash drawing of the *Cleopatra* by Nicholas Pocock following its launch in Bristol in 1779.

Continue walking west, turning left down Polygon Lane footpath to Hope Chapel Hill. Turn right and right again into Hope Square.

9

Hope Square

In 1831 Richard Boucher Callender is recorded as living here in Hope Square. His paternal grandparents married in Barbados in 1773 and his father Clement was baptised in the island in 1774. Richard was articled to a Bristol attorney by his widowed mother Elizabeth Lancaster of Hotwells. He married Sarah Grundon in Clifton in 1827.

Richard Boucher Callender, friend of Charles Pinney, lived here in Hope Square.

Richard used his legal expertise successfully to counterclaim against his aunt Mary Jane Callender for the compensation on Hopefield Plantation in Barbados on the basis of a mortgage. The claim was for 154 slaves in Barbados with a compensation payout of £3334 6s 2d.

This small covered entry links
Granby Hill with Hope Square.

PLEASE MIND YOUR HEAD

Richard had an interesting friendship with Charles Pinney who was Mayor of Bristol in 1832. Youngest son of John Pinney, Charles was born on 29 April 1793 at the Georgian House in Great George Street *(see walk 4)* and succeeded to the Pinney estates in Nevis. He was a Bristol merchant and slave owner in partnership with Robert Edward Case. Their firm received £3572 compensation for their slaves' emancipation.

The Bristol Riots of 1831 took place after the House of Lords rejected the second Reform Bill, which had aimed to abolish some of the rotten boroughs and give Britain's fast growing industrial towns such as Bristol, Manchester, Birmingham, Bradford and Leeds greater representation in the House of Commons.

Bristol had been represented in the House of Commons since 1295, but by 1830 only 6000 of the 104,000 population had the vote. Local magistrate Sir Charles Wetherell, a strong opponent of the Bill, visited Bristol to open the new Assize Courts, on 29 October 1831. He threatened to imprison participants in a disturbance going on outside, and an angry mob chased him to the Mansion House in Queen Square. The magistrate escaped in disguise but Charles Pinney and his officials were besieged in the Mansion House.

The rioters numbering about 500 to 600 young men persevered for three days, during which the palace of Robert Gray the Bishop of Bristol, the Mansion House, and private homes and property were looted and destroyed, along with demolition of much of the gaol. Work on the Clifton Suspension Bridge was halted and Isambard Kingdom Brunel was sworn in as a special constable.

Finally the military, until then in a state of indecision, charged and fired on the crowd. About sixteen persons were killed, or perished in the flames, and one hundred were wounded or injured. Captured rioters were tried by a special commission in Bristol in January 1832, and four were executed and 22 transported.

On 25 October 1832 Charles Pinney was put on trial in the court of King's Bench, charged with neglect of duty in his office as Mayor of Bristol during the riots and Richard Boucher Callender was called as a witness. The trial lasted seven days the jury returned a verdict of not guilty, asserting that Pinney 'acted according to the best of his judgment, with zeal and personal courage.'

Exit from Hope Square through the small covered entry at the top left hand corner to access Granby Hill.

Granby Place, Granby Hill

Sometime during the following decade Richard Boucher Callender moved with his family into a property in Granby Hill, possibly number 63. The 1841 census shows him to be a forty-year-old solicitor living here with his wife Sarah (also forty) and his daughter Margaretta nine and sons Richard six and Henry four plus one female servant.

In the course the nxt decade Sarah died and Richard is recorded in 1851 living with all his children still at home, with a couple of visiting relations on his mother's side, Caroline Lancaster thirty-seven and Sarah Lancaster aged six and two female servants.

Climb up Granby Hill and turn left at the top to arrive back at Wellington Terrace.

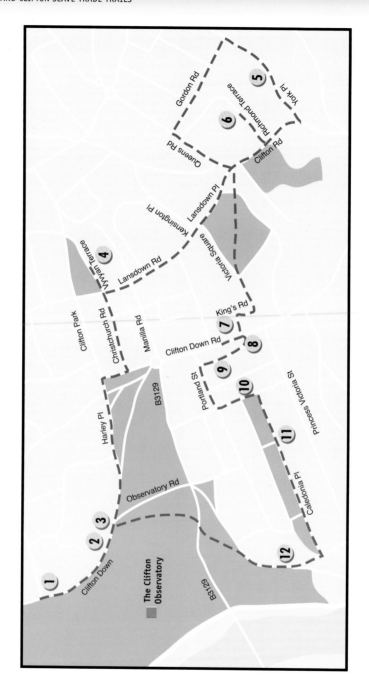

TRAIL SIX

We begin the walk near the top of Clifton Down Road by Engineers House stopping to consider Litfield House and 2 Litfield Place on route.

During the first half of the eighteenth century Clifton on the hill remained grazing land and market gardens with the bulk of the population still living down by the river. A few of Bristol's most prosperous merchants built mansions in and around the village of Clifton, moving from the pollution and cramped houses of the old city to clearer air on the hill. Some of these mansions still survive along Clifton Down Road.

Peeking from behind high hedges along the length of airy Clifton Down Road are mansions built by wealthy merchants who could afford to escape the pollution of the old city.

1

Engineers House

Engineers House, previously known as Camp House, was built in 1830 on The Promenade, Clifton Down, by Charles Dyer for Charles Pinney. It is now used as offices.

John Pinney *(see walk 4)* was determined his sons should succeed him in the slave plantation sugar business and gave them a good education. John Frederick was required to spend some time in the island of Nevis before settling as a Bristol merchant. Part of the estate was transferred to him and a few new slaves were purchased to increase the existing workforce. Unfortunately he did not inherit his

Engineers House on The Promenade, Clifton Down was built for Charles Pinney in 1830.

father's acumen for business and proved to be a disappointment.

John's second son, Azariah, died young. Ultimately it was Pinney's youngest son Charles, who inherited his father's trading skills and secured the future of the business. When Charles became manager he inherited a share of his father's fortune which he increased substantially by his own business dealings.

Before John Pinney's death in 1818, aged nearly eighty, he gave his Bristol house at 7, Great George Street to Charles. At the time John Pinney's assets were valued at £340,000 (about £17 million today). Charles became Mayor of Bristol in 1831 and was in office during the Bristol

Charles Pinney Mayor of Bristol during the Reform Bill riots of 1831.

Riots *(see walk 3)*. He retained possession of the house in Great George Street, after moving to Clifton, selling it in 1861.

When slavery ended in 1834 Charles Pinney still owned property and slaves in the island of Nevis. He claimed around £36,000 as his share of compensation for slaves he owned outright and for other slaves on plantations where he and his partners were owed money from loans they had made on the properties.

Litfield House, home of linen merchant Henry Bush and his family.

1 Litfield Place (Litfield House)

Many of those involved in the Africa trade were linen merchants. Henry Bush, who lived at Litfield House, was a magistrate and merchant who employed about 1500 men in the Great Western Cotton Works in Bristol. He was related to the Hilhouse family of Bristol and had an interest in a West

Indian plantation. His cousin George Hilhouse was awarded £7247 6s compensation for the loss of 341 slaves in Barbados.

This former slave house on Barbados makes an interesting contrast with the Clifton slave owners' mansions.

The 1841 census shows Henry Bush aged forty living at Litfield House Clifton with his wife Eleanor and Sarah Hilhouse, both also forty. Litfield House is now a Medical Centre providing private consulting rooms.

2 Litfield Place, home to slave owner Charles Thomas Alleyne and his family.

3

2 Litfield Place

In 1820, Charles Thomas Alleyne, of 2 Litfield Place, inherited the 636 acre estates of Porters and Mount Standfast in Barbados from his father John Forster Alleyne. At the time the estates were valued at £44,264. Charles continued to expand his holdings and in 1823 he bought Seniors, a 158 acre estate in St Joseph. Two years later he paid the Chancery Court £35,714 for the 365 acre Dunscombe estate in St Thomas.

He eventually received compensation of £18,128 1s for the loss of 865 slaves and died here at Litfield Place on 4 April 1872.

Continue along Clifton Down bearing left into Harley Place. Cross the junction with Canynge Road to enter Clifton Park, turning right into Clifton Down Road and first left into Christchurch Road. Continue to the cross roads with Lansdown Road and walk ahead into Vyvyan Terrace where number 3 appears on your left.

4

3 Vyvyan Terrace

West Indies plantation owners and their children tended to intermarry with other families involved in the Africa trade, and none more than Lucy Tobin (née Oliver) who lived at 3 Vyvyan Terrace. The daughter of Thomas Oliver, the former Governor of Massachusetts, she was recipient with other heirs of £1984 (£170,300) compensation in respect of Friars Hill plantation in Antigua.

Lucy Tobin (née Oliver) daughter of Thomas Oliver, the former Governor of Massachusetts lived at 3 Vyvyan Terrace (first door on the left).

Thomas Oliver's father and grandfather before him had owned property in Antigua. Thomas's four daughters, Lucy, Mary, Harriet and Penelope all married into slave owning families. Lucy married Henry Hope Tobin at St Augustine's in Bristol on 22 November 1798, son of James Tobin and Elizabeth Webbe, the daughter of Nevis slave-owner George Webbe.

James Tobin, a Nevis planter had been John Pinney's partner and had engaged in a public debate with James Ramsay over slavery in 1785. Interestingly, one of Tobin's sons, James Webbe Tobin, became friendly with Coleridge and Wordsworth. A prospective 'Pantisocrat', he later contributed five poems to the second volume of Southey's *Annual Anthology* and urged Southey to produce a third. In September 1807 he married Jane Mallet and from 1809 till his death he lived in Nevis, campaigning against cruelty to slaves.

Another son, Lieutenant George Tobin, 'an unusual naval officer of wide interests and an enquiring mind', sailed with Captain Bligh on *The Bounty*, and kept a journal of the voyage providing an unusually balanced portrait of Bligh. Tobin was also a gifted water colour artist and on the two-year voyage produced a sketchbook containing 84 pictures, several pen and ink sketches and a map of the Torres Strait.

On 31 May 1798 Lucy's sister Mary married Charles Anthony Partridge of Cotham Lodge, Cotham Park Bristol who was successful in a slave claim of £1984 (£170,300), and Harriet married Henry Haynes from another Barbadian slave owning family who were also hugely successful in compensation claims.

Exceptional cruelty to the slaves in Antigua prompted an article in the *Anti-Slavery Reporter* on 25 October 1831:

'... the cruelties of some of the planters, in Antigua, had arrived at so alarming a height as to make it necessary for the public authorities of the Island to adopt measures to put down such flagrant and wanton enormities, and particularly calling upon him to institute an inquiry into the treatment of the slaves on Friar's Hill estate, the property of Captain Haynes of the Royal Navy.'

'... a young pregnant slave had been brutally treated by the manager of that estate, and afterwards confined in a horrid dungeon, from which she was only released when the *manager was courteously informed by a magistrate, that he should be under the necessity of visiting the estate to ascertain the truth or falsehood of the rumour.'*

'The Governor's correspondent further informed him, that on this same estate were erected two dungeons, ingeniously contrived for the torture of slaves, one of very small dimensions and so imperfectly ventilated as to produce the most suffocating effects; and another where the slaves lie on their backs with their limbs stretched out, and loaded with iron fetters, in one or other of which, slaves had been confined for months in succession, and one for two years or more.'

Return to the crossroads and turn left into Lansdown Road. Follow this all the way down to the junction with Queens Road and turn left. Turn right into Gordon Road and walk down to the junction with York Place and turn right.

5

York Place

Three families associated with the slave trade are featured among the residents of York Place; Johnson, Allwood and Trotman. Particularly poignant is the case of Elizabeth Johnson who had just one slave in Barbados and received compensation for £19 8s 4d. Elizabeth lived at number 1, the only house in the terrace which no longer exists.

A couple of doors away at number 3 lived Reverend Robert Allwood who had 202 slaves in British Guiana and received a substantial compensation payment of £10,543 12s 1d (£905,000). He was born in Kingston Jamaica in 1803, educated at Eton and Cambridge and later became a colonial clergyman in Australia. In May 1835 he married

When he lived here at 3 York Place, Reverend Robert Allwood, was compensated for the loss of 202 slaves in British Guiana. He later became vicar of St James' church, Sydney.

Anna Rebecca, daughter of Joseph Bush of Martinique and sailed to Australia in July 1839 to become vicar of St James' church, Sydney, a post he held for forty-four years from 1840-1884.

Number 7 was home to Ann Trotman and her daughter whose fortunes derived from Barbados.

At number 7 lived Ann Trotman (née Hamilton) who had inherited compensation for Bulkeley's and Carmichael plantations in Barbados as heir of her late husband. Ann married Thomas Clarke Trotman in St Michael, Barbados, in October 1794 and bore eight children.

Thomas Clarke Trotman had received £18,012 (£1.4 million) in compensation with other family members receiving the following payments: Joseph Trotman, £9006 (£773,100); Simon Lee Trotman £9006 (£773,100).

Ann Trotman (junior) of the same address received £348 (£29,870). By 1861 she is recorded as still unmarried and living here with her mother and two female servants. Interestingly her occupation is given as 'Railway Debenture Holder', demonstrating how slave trade compensation money helped fund Britain's Industrial Revolution. Ann remained a spinster and died here on 28 August 1887.

At the end of York Place turn right up Clifton Road and right again into Richmond Terrace.

Richmond Terrace

John James Vidal was born in Westmor-land Parish Jamaica in 1763. He owned 173 slaves on the Berkshire Hall plantation and had been a member of the Jamaican Assembly before he came to live at 34 Richmond Terrace where he died in 1823.

John was barely two years old when his father died and his mother and stepsisters perished in the devastating hurricane of 3 October 1780. Differing accounts about that dreadful night have survived. One recalls how John saved his first cousin, Elizabeth Allwood, (a girl he was to marry seven years later) by helping her cling to a spar when the tidal wave engulfed their house in Savanna la Mar, sweeping them into the sea.

John James Vidal had 173 slaves on the Berkshire Hall plantation in Jamaica when he moved here to 34 Richmond Terrace.

Another tells of Elizabeth aged nearly six and her two brothers of four and eleven being saved by their faithful black nurse who, with the help of another slave, rushed them to higher ground as the waters rose. Around 400 souls perished as a result of the hurricane and tidal wave. Of the 60 or 70 houses in the town not one was left standing.

Maria Pearce Hall and her sisters Herriot and Lucretia, residents of Richmond Terrace, each received compensation for the loss of their slaves in the Leeward Island of St Kitts.

Jane Caroline Vidal, John James's daughter, married slave owner Herbert Jarrett James who was awarded compensation for seventeen enslaved people in St John, Jamaica. John Grant Wilson who lived at 17 Richmond Terrace was unsuccessful in his claim for £1380 14s 4d in respect of 63 slaves in Barbados. Maria Pearce Hall and her sisters Herriot and Lucretia, also residents of Richmond Terrace, fared rather better, each receiving compensation of £1978 (£169,800) in respect of 119 slaves in the Leeward Island of St Kitts. August 1st is Emancipation Day on St Kitts and celebrated as a public holiday.

Return to Clifton Road and turn right to the junction and bear left to walk diagonally across Victoria Square, exiting into Boyce's Avenue. Turn right into King's Road and follow the road round to the junction with Clifton Down Road. A little further on the right is Mortimer House.

7

Mortimer House

Mortimer House has recently undergone complete restoration. It was home to Richard Hart Davis, a Bristol merchant trading to the West Indies, and a partner from 1794 in Harford's Bank in the city. Hart Davis joined the Society of Merchant Venturers in 1803. His commercial speculations were 'very fortunate' and in 1810 he was reported to have made £200,000 by 'getting possession of all the Spanish wool in the kingdom'.

By 1813 he was at his zenith and Joseph Farington, the eighteenth-century English landscape painter and diarist, recorded:

Richard Hart Davis, merchant and banker.

'Hart Davis had not 20 or 25 years ago a thousand pounds in the world, and is now supposed to be worth from 3 to, £500,000. He is an exception to the general character of

Mortimer House, just one of the luxury mansions owned by Richard Hart Davis.

Bristol merchants as he lives at a large expense, has a house at Mortimer Road Clifton and another near it; one in Grosvenor Square, London, and another in its vicinity. His collection of pictures it is supposed, cost him £100,000'.

From Mortimer House cross Clifton Down Road where Rodney House appears on the left.

Rodney House

This house was home to James Evan Baillie a merchant and banker of London and Bristol. The son of Evan Baillie of Dochfour and Mary Gurley of St Vincent, James became a major recipient of compensation for the loss of Caribbean slaves. In total he owned 2418 slaves across British Guiana, Grenada, St Kitts, St Vincent and Trinidad and received £83, 632 18s 11d. in compensation payouts.

Rodney House, home to West Indies merchant and Bristol banker James Evan Baillie.

Baillie founded a highly successful West Indies merchant firm in Bristol, in premises that later became the Old Bank. His family moved from being successful West Indies planters to bankers in Bristol. The Old Bank was originally set up in 1750 in Broad Street *(see walk 2)* and was one of the banks established with slave trade money that eventually merged into the National Westminster Bank.

Despite his extensive possessions in the Caribbean James never went abroad, but owned a large fleet of trading ships and cultivated a network of young Scots employed on his plantations. He acquired Redland Court mansion (now

Bristol High School) and 150 acres of surrounding farmland from Sir Richard Vaughan in 1829, following Vaughan's bankruptcy. Vaughan had mortgaged the estate to Elton, Baillie & Co. (the Old Bank) in 1823.

Baillie died in June 1863, having instructed that £55,000, raised in part from the sale of estates in Gloucestershire and Glamorgan, should be divided among ten individuals, who were possibly his illegitimate children.

Head north up Clifton Down Road and turn left into Rodney Place.

9

Rodney Place

Some of the terraced houses in Rodney Place are incorporated into the present day Rodney Hotel. George Cunningham who lived here owned 484 slaves in Jamaica and received £9921 17s 1d. compensation. Eliza Cunningham owned 8 slaves in Tobago and received £202 6s 7d, while James Cunningham with 1950 slaves in St Vincent and Tobago received the princely sum of £40,199 7s 1d.

The terrace incorporating the Rodney Hotel was formerly home to George Cunningham who, along with other members of the family, received extensive compensation payouts.

Walk to the end of Rodney Place and turn left into Portland Street and second left into The Mall to reach Clifton Assembly Rooms on the left.

For over 190 years The Assembly Rooms have been home to The Clifton Club, one of the most socially exclusive organisations in Bristol.

10

Clifton Assembly Rooms, 22 The Mall

The Clifton Club purchased the old Clifton Assembly Rooms and Hotel. For over 190 years it has been one of the most socially exclusive organisations in Bristol, with a long and well documented link with the Society of Merchant Venturers, many members of which are still also members of the Clifton Club.

Membership must be gained on the invitation and recommendation of at least two members of good standing who have each known the candidate for at least three years. Historically the club's membership has included the heads of major Bristol businesses, local landed gentry, and the higher echelons of the professions.

This oil painting by Rolinda Sharples depicts people arriving at the Clifton Assembly Rooms and preparing to enter the ballroom.

Pass the Assembly Rooms on your left, turn right into Caledonia Place and walk about halfway down to number 31.

Nathaniel Cave, who lived at 31 Caledonia Place, was a member of the wealthy family having investments in banking, the glass industry and Caribbean plantations.

11

31 Caledonia Place

Nathaniel Cave, who lived here at 31 Caledonia Place, was paid compensation of £3,615 (£310,300). The Cave family had investments in banking, the glass industry and Caribbean plantations. A number of references to family members in the records of slave trade compensation include John Cave of

Brentry House, Westbury-on-Trym who received £1984 (£170,300) and Stephen Cave of Cleve Hill (north east of Bristol) who owned 675 slaves in Jamaica and received £13, 795 4s 10d. His second son married into the Cumberbatch family of Barbados where the Cave family owned St Nicholas Abbey plantation in Saint Peter, Barbados, one of only three genuine Jacobean mansions surviving west of Europe. It is similar to the English Jacobean manor houses of the first half of the seventeenth century, the period between the Tudor and Georgian styles, beginning in the reign of James I.

St Nicholas Abbey, the plantation house in Saint Peter, Barbados owned by members of the Cave family.

Walk to the bottom of Caledonia Place into Sion Hill and up to the distinctive looking house on the right called St. Vincent Rocks.

St Vincent Rocks

Still popularly known as St Vincent Rocks, this fashionable Georgian dwelling on Sion Hill overlooking Avon George and Clifton Suspension Bridge was owned by Josias Jackson who also owned a similarly named property on Rutland Vale, one of the three main estates in the Caribbean island of St Vincent.

This fashionable Sion Hill dwelling (seen on the left with green covered balconies) was owned by Josias Jackson, heir to five plantations on St Vincent.

Heir to five plantations in St Vincent, Jackson took part in the Carib War of 1795. The conflict pitted large numbers of British military forces against a coalition of Black Carib, runaway slaves and French forces for control of the island.

In 1803 he settled near Southampton and attracted attention to himself through lavish hospitality and being colonel of the local volunteers. He died in St Vincent on 30 August 1819, *'one of the most worthy and polished men that ever adorned the island.'* His will was in dispute until 1834, due to a bonded debt incurred in 1817, but eventually his plantations were divided among his sons.

Jackson was MP for Southampton from 1807 to 1812. A memorial recalls that: *'During the period he sat in Parliament, though unaccustomed to speak in the House, when some West India regulations were in agitation, he made a clear and comprehensive speech on the state of affairs in those islands; in which he took occasion to explain the general benevolent treatment of slaves there, and evinced with great perspicuity, how humanely, kindly, and even liberally, they were supported by a large portion of their masters.'*

Walk north across Clifton Down (crossing the B3129) and turn left at the next road junction to return to the start.

An eighteenth-century prospect of Avon Gorge.